For my Mam and Diann, two equally amazing women who never stopped encouraging me to breathe life into my soul. My gratitude knows no boundaries.

Preface

I'll often say that writing this book has been the biggest work of my life. But really, the work I've done has brought me to experience some of the most amazing times I've ever had, even in my moments of doubt, fear, pain and confusion for not knowing how the truth of my story would eventually appear on paper. The biggest work of my life, instead, was living through recovery from Anorexia Nervosa; this was the time when I was faced with the truth of ME, which has now become the contents of this book.

After I was first diagnosed, I didn't initially have the vision of one day writing a book on this topic. When treatment started in July 2008, six weeks after diagnosis, I started writing on a personalized blog. The blog was with the intent of keeping my loved ones—who mostly lived outside of Ireland—up to date on how my recovery was progressing. I also wished for my suffering to be 'purposeful'. And the only purpose I believed the eating disorder could have was helping other patients. This was an uplifting notion: inspiring individuals as I faced my own treatment head-on. But as soon as my healing started, I had to block out the thoughts of there being other sufferers in the world. It was too painful to think of patients enduring similar experiences as I was. Also I had come to be sitting too deep in my own dark world. The blog had transformed itself into my coping mechanism, whether or not the outside world was following my words or learning from my pain. Recovery was suddenly only about me.

When I started to see the light, the longing I once had to share my blog, started to reappear, and it was stronger than before. I wished for others to see what can come of a life, if a sufferer uses not only their determination and strength to fight the illness, but also their spirit, their dreams, their passions and their desires to live out their own truth, the truth that has become suppressed under the eating disorder. I needed to inspire others to heal themselves from the root of their illness, so that the suppression they have been experiencing throughout their entire lives can be released in order for a true spirit to come to life and to be a part of this world.

With this wish in my heart, I set off from Ireland to travel. I carried my story inside, without speaking of it. And sixteen months later, in August of 2010, the desire to share it with others brought me back to my hometown in Arklow, Co. Wicklow. I couldn't ignore this deep longing anymore. I was even feeling to be a hoard. I felt selfish for living my life, for being here in the world and not actually taking the time and effort to create something that could help individuals, in whatever way possible. So I put my travels on hold and permitted myself to do the work I felt I was destined to do in this life and I started creating something that would set the words in my blog free.

On returning, I was convinced my blog would be the contents of the book. So I started diving back into my archive and found myself swimming in past emotions and personal torture once again. I never realized that I'd been so expressive and so accurate about the process of my personal journey through anorexia. However REAL my blog was, I felt it wasn't meant to be the contents of the book. The blog was, instead, my own place of research. It contained alongside my own emotions described in detail, the actual workings of the eating disorder, of addiction in general and the physical and mental connection. I found my blog to be teaching me what I needed to know in order for this current book to become a story revealing the workings of anorexia interpreted through the eyes of the soul. I realized, during my weeks of research, that, even though I had an amazingly enlightening therapist guiding me, I was my own teacher. I was the writer of the blog and the contents of the blog came to me by connecting with my truth, and this connection had only been made possible through battling anorexia. So my story was to be an example of what an individual can gain, by not running away from self-healing, but confronting that illness and the destructive demon inside with at least 100% of personal power.

I'm not a graduate and I have never studied intensely. I'm not a poet, or a journalist, or a columnist. I'm none of these things. And I never thought I'd ever be capable of writing anything. Years ago I never wanted to read books, let alone write books! Before being diagnosed, I knew nothing about eating disorders, and very little about myself. But healing brought me to research my own personal world, and with that, the illness and the workings of the mind and the body, in order to feel and feed the soul. Living through the illness and carrying out my own so-called research (and recording what I'd encountered on my blog) made me eligible to have created this book without a doubt in my mind of its truth and accuracy.

Sixteen months passed by, between reaching a recovered state (April 2009) and actually sitting down to create this book (August 2010), and I'd learned a great deal more. I saw myself and the illness through eyes that didn't despise anorexia. I wasn't afraid of having to dive into that space in my head and relive the entire endurance. It was painful at the best of times, on every level of my being and often I thought I'd never feel ME again. The depths I had to reach back into were far out of sight, yet close in feeling, once I managed to touch on those weeds again. And it was all to make my wish come true. It's been a blessing that I followed through my longing and it's a gift that I'm now sharing it.

Since finishing the third draft in June 2011, I've been looking more deeply into the path other patients have followed. It's become clear to me that the majority is forced only to cure their physical ailments. The outside world sees the manifestation of the illness, but doesn't know the actual root. The world sees the effect, but doesn't realize the cause. With any sufferer, one can only heal their hurts and rid their souls of their demons, if they start from the root of their existence. As human beings, the root of us is not our body, it is our spirit, our soul. I've realized how lucky I am to have healed in this manner and not to have been 'cured' by some magic potion that would stabilize only my physical self without ever knowing and understanding the cause and the reason for anorexia to have come into my life. I feel it's even more essential for sufferers, for their families and for professionals too, to be open to the truth that lies behind each and every eating disorder and to realize that spiritual healing should be given at least as much importance as medically curing the sufferer.

Healing as a whole, must include our spirit. It's the only true way for patients to establish a solid ground of spiritual trust within themselves. This trust is what a recovered individual can use as guidance throughout their lives. Because challenges will definitely be experienced along the way, but it's the connection with the spirit that can catch the individual if they stumble and fall, whilst facing those challenges. Spiritual trust in one's self can prevent excruciating relapses from happening, even if the surrounding world suddenly shatters the solidity within and causes old habits to resurface. With such a connection, suffering will never be endured as intensely as before.

Sharing my story will hopefully inspire others, those who are either professionally or personally dealing with an eating disorder, to at least turn their heads in the direction of alternative soulful deep healing. I know it's impossible to change the world with one story, but if I manage to help a few people, by making this small contribution and adding spirit, strength, love and life to the endurance of any individual, then for me, it's the start of a change, however small it may seem in the eyes of the world.

Acknowledgements

This is a moment to acknowledge the people who were close to me whilst I was living through the experience of recovering from Anorexia Nervosa. Regardless of how deep into my own world I travelled, as the journey of healing evolved, recovery itself would never have been possible without support from outsiders; my family, friends and professionals. It's clear that this book would never have been written without healing, and healing would never have been the case without that support. So these few lines, in their simple expression yet their deep meaning, are for all of those who believed in my strength from the very start of my journey and who continued to encourage, guide and follow me throughout my recovery. These few lines are for those who never stopped loving me and who never started judging me based on the condition I was suffering from. My gratitude for their acceptance of ME in that condition, to this day, remains endless.

I wish to mention my siblings Emma, Orla, Eileen and Sean, who I consider to be my closest family; they never showed an ounce of fear or rejection for who I was, what I was becoming or what I was experiencing. They accepted, they encouraged and they offered me love without bounds, even when I had nothing to offer. My Dad somehow knew the course of action to take, when my diagnosis was revealed and for this, I could not give him more thanks. My cousin, best friend and soul mate Sandra, is someone who has always fully heard the depth behind the seemingly unimportant words I have spoken and written, ever since we were young girls. She's a star and an inspiration in herself. My cousin Mark came falling out of the sky when I needed somebody with a subtle force and a deeper understanding of the illness. How happy I was, and still am, for him to have 'fallen'. The role he took upon himself didn't stop when I was recovered; he also played an important part in wrapping this story up nicely with a REAL projection of what's inside, using his graphic eye, creativity and inside scope on what this book entails.

My aunt and uncle, John and Ann, were never far when my Mam needed to release her worries; as being the witness to her daughters' suffering inevitably brought her suffering too. From my aunt and uncle however, she received back-up without question. My auntie Brigid has, since the start of healing, become a guiding light and always appeared when I needed her most, to this day she still does. My cousin Naomi and brother-in-laws Marcel and Arno, followed the process of my recovery in their own way and did their best to support my closest family. Trish and Ed, I thank dearly. They let me feel their love from the other end of the earth and their absence made their support all the more empowering. Jason made me realize that love does travel in spirit, even if the body doesn't permit the actual movement. My friends in Holland; Janneke, Natasja, Jorien and Wendy, were uplifting, simply for the fact that they never turned their back on me, even when I was unrecognizable to them. The travelling spirit of Kelly, touched my heart. Our connection has developed and strengthened over time.

A special mention goes to our family friend Julie, who places her positive spirit ahead of everything she does in life. She used this spirit to support and uplift myself and especially my Mam. She will always know where extra life and power needs to be injected. And when this complete manuscript was in need of that extra life, she played her part in bringing it to where it is today.

Dr. Buggle and Dr. McCabe did everything they could to help my treatment. I felt cared for, by them both, even though I felt they had little reason to. They have given me a place of support and understanding, where I will always be able to turn without ever feeling a sense of shame for any issues I may be facing in life. This is a treasure. As is the contact with Ralph, my acupuncturist. Since connecting with him, wherever I go in the world, he will always be 'my acupuncturist'. The amazing work he did taught me such subtle lessons on the power of alternative medicine combined with the power of spirit. He'll never realize that as he was treating me, he was also teaching me. The company I worked for in Holland, D-Reizen, need to be recognized for their efficiency in helping practical matters throughout the whole uncertain timeframe of my recovery. They did their duty without expecting anything in return.

I would like to honour my therapist and voice of wisdom, Diann, who has since become my dearest soul friend. Throughout healing she was the bridge between my ill self and my true self. Acknowledging the role she played is through writing this book. My Mam is placed in a similar light. She was, and still is, the voice of home. Her strength gives way to a voice of understanding and full acceptance of the situations that have led to suffering. It leads to her own wisdom that enables her to accept me for who I was, for who I am today and for who I'm yet to become.

Publisher and dear friend Lorraine receives my deepest appreciation for recognizing the spirit in my story and in my writing. Also her courage needs to be noted for not letting the distance between India and Ireland be a reason for withholding this story. May the love and hard work she does, continue to connect authors and readers.

Lastly, I give thanks to the place on earth I've found where magic can happen: it's the Irish soil that supports the desk in my room and it stands in front of the window. It's that special place where my words can be expressed, my thoughts can be at peace and my spirit can be free.

Introduction

It's nothing short of a miracle that I'm able to bring this story to your hands, for the simple fact that, of all the dreams I've had throughout my life, this is the dream I never envisioned to happen so suddenly, so passionately and only made possible through battling the illness of Anorexia Nervosa. This is the eating disorder I was diagnosed with on the 9th of June 2008. It felt to have come falling out of the sky, knocking me for six and forcing me to discover who I was and what substance I'm made of.

The words within this book are ones telling of my tale, from my current twenty-seven-year-old perspective. It's one containing tears of joy and pain, depths of wisdom and innocence, adventures of the outer and inner world and dreams already lived and currently still unfolding. A huge portion of soul is injected, so the words will reach the place they're meant to, which is also the place from which they originate: the heart.

The way in which I've chosen to express my story is by perceiving my past through the eyes of the illness. I review how and where the destructive force of the disorder was able to take ahold of me. The power comes to light by looking deep into life situations, circumstances, relationships and personal choices. At times it may appear as though my memories were unhappy ones and that the choices I made were the wrong ones. But it needs to be as clear as the light of day that HAPPINESS is what my life has always been filled with.

Through this story, I wish to shine a light on just how much every individual—even those who never 'welcome' anorexia into their lives—can learn and grow by taking the plunge into their subconscious mind and seeing their own truth. Every single person who walks this earth, has elements of the soul that could very well remain concealed throughout their time here on earth. The saying goes 'everybody has a song to sing', which is something that is more real than anybody could ever imagine. However not everybody chooses to find that song and to sing it loud and clear. This is why, me bringing my story to your hands, is a miracle. Because this is my song and it's my time to sing.

The illness set me on the course of my subconscious search for something deeper. I never knew that for the first twenty-five years of my life, I was searching so passionately. I only ever found out this truth, by having landed myself in my current 'status', which I class not as somebody who has survived anorexia but instead as somebody who has thrived throughout the developing stages, the endurance of the illness and the recovery.

There are no promises that by the end you'll feel happy, sad, confused, educated, deflated, entertained or even hungry for food or for life. But the one thing that I can promise you is that by choosing to connect with me here and now and opening up your heart, letting go of the search for explanations and by trusting that my revelations will also becomes yours, the magic that I found will come to light.

Part I

1

BEFORE OCTOBER 1992

The starting point of one's life, usually, is birth. But for me, it always felt to have been October of 1992. For a particular month of a particular year to be given such importance, could be an indication that something major happened. However, the change that came about, the one that marked this month as being so significant for somebody who was only nine years old at the time, wouldn't necessarily appear to others as being a huge ordeal. But to me, it was. My family and I moved away from my home country of Ireland to start a new life in Holland. It was a new beginning for my three sisters, my Mam and I—my parents had only recently separated, so my Dad wasn't a part of the move. My Mam's choice to move was with the intention of starting a new life and freeing our family of her past. This was never a secret. Regardless if it did or didn't offer us the desired freedom, I'll always feel that leaving behind a marriage that was dominated by the absence of the other half was both a courageous as well as a wise move.

Home life in Ireland revolved around a person who was never there. How strange to feel an absence so strongly when my sisters and I had no clue really what it would be like if he were to have been a permanent presence in our lives. We based our wishes for my Dad's homecoming on the odd occasions when he would pass through. Those were times when things changed. I'm still not too sure if it was for good or bad. All I know is that, as a young girl, the drinking and the pub visits showed me his fondness and excitement towards life. It made him happy and so it made the home life happy—from what I can remember. It wasn't until much later I realized the association of happiness with alcohol was actually a representation of something far deeper than 'simple pleasures'. It was something deeper within his life, as well as mine. There was never recognition of his addiction however; it was simply ignored because he left again to work abroad for an undetermined length of time. Taking leave after his visits meant he was taking the addiction with him too. On hindsight this could have been a blessing in disguise, but at the time it didn't feel to be. As for my sisters and I, we never stopped missing him intensely and the tears we cried were mostly for him: for either having to say goodbye or for wanting him to come home. I'll never forget one of my sisters speaking about the smallest stain on her pillow. She referred to it as being the tear she'd cry each night for missing our Da.

That sadness never stopped me from seeing his life as something inspiring. I envied it even! I recall an early memory from when I was seven years old. I spoke with him on a particular day, when he was passing through. I wanted to pick his brain. I stood before him in the living room, I strained my neck to look up at him—my beautiful, strong and independent Daddy. As I gazed, I asked him what it was like to be working in faraway countries (at that time—1990—he was working in France). The only thing that stayed with me was my own eagerness to find out how I could have that kind of life too. I found the act of working abroad to be such a courageous one. I envied his position in that big wide world. I was eager to hear about the people he was meeting and how he coped with the language. At the age of seven I was so amazed. He was my motivator and was living a dream that seemed so out of reach for me. He was living something that was extra special and unique. This only meant that I saw no flaws, I saw no addiction, I saw only amazement and was so proud to be his daughter.

His lifestyle gave me reason to believe that travel would free the spirit; especially spirits that would be inclined to feel trapped in a life that wasn't suiting. This is what his travels represented in my eyes. Travel freed HIS spirit and therefore I believed travel would free MY spirit. And later, the move to Holland, of course, only strengthened my longing for free-living which I'd come to associate with travel. Freedom is travel.

***

Could I think bigger at that age? I was driven, determined and motivated as a child. I was independent, I was strong and I was a go-getter. I saw the world as being my Dad's oyster and so I wanted it to be mine, too! But as a child, how big is the world you see and feel you must conquer? As far back as I can remember my world was my home. And this home sat in a house that offered five people an environment where masses of emotions would be ever-merging: 139 Fernhill.

Mam did all she could to create the perfect loving homely environment. But how could one person sustain so much? My Mam was only human! Who was going to look after HER? Was there a man? No. Was there a nanny? No. Babysitter? No. Could I? Yes, I felt I could take on the responsibility of my Mam's happiness, which was the responsibility of my small world sitting within the four walls of our home. I could act out the independence I knew I naturally owned. I could provide care and love for the one who needed it most.

My independence brought me to be alone in fulfilling the secret desire I had of taking care of my Mam. By living and acting in a manner that would make her happy, I was subconsciously bearing the weight of her pain. It was the pain I'd never associated with the absence of my Dad. However, I was able to feel her unhappiness because of the thin skin I owned. I wouldn't tell anybody what I secretly wanted to achieve within my little world. There was no need for this. Because I was strong, I was a big thinker and dreamer. And in these big dreams I was going to eventually touch the hearts and souls of those in the big wide world. But I first was going to touch the hearts and souls of those I loved most. I had to act on a smaller scale until I was grown up enough to act on a bigger one. Subconsciously I was healing my world, by healing my Mam.

To take away a mother's pain would give me the purpose in my, so far, short life. How to do this as a child though? Could I act in every which way possible to prove I was a good girl? Yes, I could. But as a young girl, that's about the extent of what I could do. Anything else was beyond my capabilities. Of course, unaware of this fact I was. And so, I always felt as if nothing I ever did would be enough to take away my mother's pain.

In the rational minds of the world, it's beyond anybody's capabilities to heal another person's heart. Still I was aiming to fill my own heart by filling my Mam's. But my Mam still wasn't smiling, no matter how good I was. My Mam still looked unhappy when I sat in the corner and kept myself busy and quiet. My Mam still dragged herself down the stairs each morning, when I told her how well I was doing at school. Nothing was making her happy.

I continued to persevere. The belief held its ground. It became the deeper meaning behind the actions I took in the world and it was a reason for living. I believed, literally with my heart and soul, that if I kept on achieving more than everybody else and if I aimed for perfection in the actions I took, my Mam would be proud and she would smile! If I was to prove to be even better than I already had been, by the things I did, this had to eventually turn my Mam's frown upside down, permanently!

So my young subconscious mind felt to have cracked the code of a lifetime: by making my Mam happy, I would also be feeling happy. This meant both our states of happiness were only experienced through my achievements. It's something upon which I came to rely, as a young girl. Having a purpose in life, gave me a sense of self-worth. So I now had a worthy purpose. It was a good cause. The goodness of this cause—the cause being my Mam's happiness and the goodness being the perfect young girl—would certainly pay off! Did it though? Did the formula that I'd fabricated, work? Did I create happiness? No. And therefore instead of succeeding, I was failing. Big time! I carried this feeling of failure from a very young age. It was deep, so nobody could see it. Nobody knew of its existence. Not even the bearer of this feeling. I had my smile, I had my bubbly personality and I had my 'independence'. Whatever was going on beneath is where it needed to stay. And that's what happened. I simply internalized my surrounding environment—without being the conscious participator. I saw an amazing world around me and I smiled to it all. Especially with the visions of Holland welcoming five more people. Life was already proving to be a massive adventure!

AFTER OCTOBER 1992

The relocation to Holland stands as a point in time that enables me
to almost chop my childhood into two parts: one part being the first
nine years in Ireland and the other being the years that followed,
up until reaching young adulthood. And by chopping my youth
in two, I can almost stand on the dividing line and be the witness
of how my feelings and rooted interpretations of life on the Irish
home front were travelling with me, as we crossed that frontier
to set up a new life in Holland. So the line was being drawn by
my mind, but truly there was no frontier, there was no division
and everything I was destined to become, by living according to
what I'd led myself to believe at such a young age, was travelling
with me.

The Dutch world showed a different way of life. It excited me
so much and I didn't feel sad to leave Ireland. My Mam, being
the strong and consistent provider of love, care and material
needs of four young girls, unknowingly was opening our eyes
to a world that's full of opportunities. She was showing us that
the world is a vast place, even if Holland is relatively close to
Ireland. In her eagerness to offer us a better quality of life, she was
unintentionally setting us up to approach life with an open mind
that would serve all four of us forever.

I recall clearly how I was able to see the differences between
the standards of living in Ireland and Holland. I remember to have
felt so lucky for living in such a beautiful wealthy country, when

all my Irish friends were still living their lives in the same manner, year after year, back in my town of origin. When we would return for short breaks, I was always reminded of how fortunate I was. Just by being able to compare the Dutch and the Irish world, I was embracing the contrasts found within the world. This experience was a big contributor to the yearning passion I've always had to travel and experience more amazement and inspiration in the big wide world. Describing the feelings I had at such a young age, shows I was a deep thinker and I'd always known how much more there was to the simple things we see in life and the seemingly harmless actions we take and decisions we make.

I find it almost shocking how I've since changed my perception of their reality. In my mind Holland has since come to stand as being a country where systematic rules, regulations and orderly functioning are wrapped up nice and neatly with a contained projection of perfection to the rest of the world. Due to the road I've since travelled, I can see how their society can feel to suppress those who are yearning to feed their souls instead of their minds. For the minority in Dutch society, who strive to live from the depth of their being, such suppression can resemble a switch that's being flicked and 'off' are the lights of the soul. Those experiencing suppression and containment are the ones in society who know and feel there's more to life than achievements linked to education, certificates and career. Those are the ones who feel dissatisfied, even when being top of the class. They have dimmed their soulful light in order to fit-in and subconsciously search for other ways that will bring into the world something deeper than the aforementioned 'certified status within society'.

If a person doesn't know themselves, is sensitive by nature and exposed to a dominant, powerful and strong society then remaining contained and suppressed becomes the drive throughout the individual's life. If a person doesn't know who they are, then they can never know how much they're being affected by their surrounding world or if it's beneficial or not for the deeper longings a person can have. If a person doesn't know their own heartfelt rules and regulations, then they can only listen and follow the rules within society.

It seems I was being introduced to a world that predicted the future life that's supposed to be lived, instead of a future that the individual chooses to create by letting their own personal desires guide them whilst ignoring what's classed as 'right or wrong' and 'good or bad' by the majority. If my current observation of Dutch life is fact or fiction, who can say! But to me, I feel it so strongly and therefore it's my own personal fact. I've since learned that it's okay to form an opinion based on personal experiences and it's only natural to not feel fitting and homing in every country in the world. But at that point in my life, Holland felt like a great place to be. It was my home.

***

So, the world around me had changed, but all that I'd created within, before the move, was still sitting inside. I still had the same behaviour, still fuelled by the same belief and I still was convinced that I was failing as a person, with the growing realization that I couldn't heal my Mam's heart by my own personal achievements. As a child it hadn't worked and, as puberty was approaching, it still wasn't working. The task of my lifetime continued to fail. My purpose felt to be vanishing. No perfection achieved and therefore a feeling of shame started to fill a space within. But that was the space I wanted to fill with my 'pride for succeeding' instead of 'shame for failing'! The desired sense of pride was meant to give me happiness. Yet in my teenage years, the achieved failure was giving me shame. Where was the happiness?

At this stage, I not only needed to continue proving to my Mam just how good I was, but to add some pride into the gap that was filled with shame, I also needed to start proving to *myself* that I was a good girl, that I still had a purpose in life and that I was a worthy cause.

How did I prove to be good, perfect and worthy? I had to continue along the same lines as I'd become accustomed to: being the best, achieving the most and aiming to stand above all else. That's where I'd find my pride! That's where the happiness lay! The shame would be diluted by proudly achieving goals!

I wasn't achieving my ultimate goal and purpose in life: healing the homely environment by my achievements. I had to bury the reality of my fear and it sat deep within me. I would never let it resurface. The strength of my subconscious was at work which meant I was aware of nothing whatsoever. All I knew was that I had to race through life and be perfect at absolutely everything and achieve, achieve and achieve some more.

I grew into the teenager who projected excitement, vibrancy and happiness to the surrounding world. In my need for perfection, I kept the longing passion alive within my heart to always prove my existence of being somewhat special and unique. But as life unfolded and the years passed by, I yearned to always be guided through my life by the force of freedom.

***

Home life on Dutch soil was filled with ups and downs—this home that was consisting no longer of four girls and my Mam. Within a year of leaving Ireland she met the love of her life. Tom. He moved in and a year later my Mam's most precious and only boy was born, Sean, the brother we never expected to have! He felt to have been the blessing we received. It was almost like he was our main reason for moving—how strange that may sound.

With seven members in the family, things weren't always easy. The relationship between my Mam and Tom was an adventurous one. There was never a dull moment and life at home was so exciting. Tom instantly became the man of the house. He was the rock, the strength, the dominant force and the one who provided for us, throughout their ten-year relationship. We had so much respect for him. When Tom first walked into our lives, we wanted to relate to him as a father—it was something we'd missed out on. But for this to have happened, both individuals involved needed to open up and embrace the other.

Back then this particular youngster was open to what the male figure was offering. He offered material needs to the extent where he himself became less abundant, as he suddenly had four girls under his wing. What a special deed that was. But deep down, love and affection is what I wanted and needed. It didn't feel to be there, due to the tough exterior he held so strongly in place. Just like my sisters, I didn't feel to have access to his heart. So still there was emptiness inside.

For any child, if a father figure isn't accessible, due to either absence in body or soul, they're missing something precious. The male energy force, if it's a permanent factor within a child's life, gives them an extra strength, an extra sense of belonging and a deeper awareness of who they are as a person. To have a mother and a father figure ever present, the child has access to their own inner psychological energies throughout their development, as within the psyche of every person there lies both feminine and masculine forces. Masculine energies, or principles, are what give the individual access to a decisive, strong, courageous and articulate nature. Goals and actions are the main drive and rational thinking is all-important. The feminine energies or principles are those of heartfelt, affectionate, truth, affection, intuition, nurturing, caring and strength. When a person feels the intuitive nature and uses courage to follow these feelings, they grant themselves access to a deeper form of guidance: it's a flow of personal wisdom that will come forth. This is something far more precious than knowledge originating from outside of the self. That guiding wisdom and the courage to use it, can only lead to self empowerment, which, in turn, can be called upon for stability, whenever the outer world threatens the inner. If either of these masculine or feminine energies happens to be lacking, due to the upbringing not to have had both providers regularly present, the inner child (that will forever sit within the soul of each person that is placed here on earth, regardless of how mature they feel or at what stage in life they find themselves) will continue the search for that missing force throughout their teenage years and even into adulthood. Of course either our mother, father or guardian can provide both masculine and feminine energies in the other's absence. One does not need to be physically present in either form to guide these energies, simple awareness on the parent or guardian's part is all that it takes.

Dealing and healing these energies—of which many aren't aware exist—will eliminate the imbalance within their soul. This is also where the work is done: deep down. The work will reveal the true self, the essence and the inner potential. With this discovery comes a comfort in duality and a realization that there is forever accessibility to both energy forces within, regardless of the people you are relating with, outside of yourself. It's just a simple shift in awareness that needs to be taken and a growing understanding that needs to come for the person who sits deep inside.

Until the moment comes for both energies to become balanced and thus for childhood wounds to be healed, a search in the outside world is what the inner child will pursue. Depending on which parent was absent in either body and/or mind, it can sometimes be sought in the step-dad or -mom, the uncle or aunt, or the family friend. As adults then, it can be sought in the form of a romantic relationship; one tries to fill the void of the missing parent, through the love of another. In relation to females who are missing the father figure: filling the empty space can be the reason for having behaviour towards the opposite sex that's classed as needy or clingy. It can also be the reason for one to speak of incompletion in the absence of a partner. It's simply a phenomenon where masculine strength, courage, decisiveness and articulation within the individual female, haven't yet been fully developed. They need those forces from the outside to bring the balance into their lives—as they haven't yet discovered the existence of both energies within their own being.

As a young teenager, my longings and desires weren't any different. My needs were normal and a father figure is what I searched for. In my search for completion I wanted to build a relationship with the new man in my Mam's life. I wanted to get close to him for love and affection. But there wasn't any response from the individual who I thought would be cut-out for the job. So for years, we all lived together so closely in a house so snug, but we couldn't have been further apart.

***

What does a girl do when she wants to get through the exterior of someone who could be her male role model? My answer was to follow the belief I'd already set up for myself, deep down, during the earliest years of my life. This was the belief that would earn myself the entitlement to feel worthy as a person. It was the voice inside my head claiming that I could attain love in the home environment, if I never failed, if I proved myself, if I achieved as much as possible and if I strived for perfection on every level. Then I would be a good girl. And who loved the good girls? Everybody! I wanted the love of the world, but from one person in particular. Tom.

There was a force outside of myself and I needed to break it down. I felt incapable of doing so, but I had to find a way! I was strong, independent and without letting the world know, I would continue to live according to the belief I'd been living by: achievement = approval = happiness = love. I took from his forces all the essentials and they only strengthened my belief and motivation to achieve more. He was strong, proud and dominant and those were the exact energies I was missing. So I adopted his energies and became a strong exterior. I used his qualities to do all that I could to make him love me. What a genius my subconscious mind was turning out to be, so early in life!

And so, as the sensitive young girl, I was stronger, more achievement oriented and more motivated than ever before. I was determined to make it big in the world. This was fantastic!

Up until the age of seventeen, Tom and I never got close. I worked hard trying to score high marks, being as good as possible and setting future goals. I never did enough though, in my own eyes. I never felt to reach the level of perfection that would offer me the approval from the male figure on the home front. Needless to say, I continued my mission. But it was proving to be impossible. Not only did I feel to be failing in his eyes (as his exterior was still solid as a rock and he still didn't praise or complement me), I then was failing in my own eyes, just for lacking his approval and praise. So if he wasn't impressed, then Mam obviously wasn't impressed! Irrational and subconscious childhood misinterpreted beliefs were suddenly of the essence: I tried to make my Mam smile by being the good girl, but I failed. Yet he made her smile so easily! I tried to make Tom proud of me by achieving, but I failed. Yet Mam made him proud so easily! Conclusion: it must all be my own fault! What a hopeless case and a pointless waste of energy this search for approval was turning out to be! But the willpower, the energy, the force and the determination would never let anything EVER get the better of me. My mission continued.

***

A sudden change occurred at the age of seventeen. A split happened between the provider of materials, Tom, and provider of love, Mam. Their relationship ended and around the same time another masculine force was found: my first love!

This changed everything. A beautiful guy suddenly started loving me! He was devoted to me and made me feel complete. He gave me a sense of belonging, a sense of being worthy and a sense of achievement. Never in my wildest dreams had I imagined to receive love from someone so precious. It showed the world that I was a good girl after all! However, it lasted for as long as the honeymoon period lasted and needing him to fill the void within my empty heart, wasn't giving the desired satisfaction. Because no matter how much he gave me, I never understood his devotion. I was in constant wonderment, 'Why does he love me so much?' This was a sure sign of low self-esteem and worthlessness on my behalf. How could I ever accept the love of someone else, if I didn't love myself? This is impossible to do and it was my natural response to reject the love he was giving.

Due to my independent streak I also felt that by having a relationship, I'd lost my independence and freedom and therefore I was, once again, failing! My need for freedom was pushing him away and as the relationship progressed I became unappreciative and took him for granted more and more. Deep down though, I couldn't live without him; losing him was another representation of failure! When he ended it abruptly, at the age of nineteen, after two years of being together, my world came crashing down. My life felt to be over and I believed so strongly that nobody would ever love me again and definitely not in the way he did. I closed my heart and took on board the words I once heard someone say, 'Following your heart only leads to pain, Niamh, so always follow your head.' And that was that! The verdict was in.

I had no more love to give, because I had none within my heart. I wasn't worthy of receiving it either, for the failure I'd become. The masculine energies I'd adopted as a teenager finally were called upon! They came to the rescue! From that moment onwards, it was Niamh against the world. My exterior was so strong, my energy was so vibrant and my enthusiasm so bright. I truly was going to make it and prove, not only to my family and to myself, but to the whole world, exactly what I was capable of!

3

AUGUST 2002

Sitting in the body of a nineteen-year-old girl there was a suppressed soul that needed the freedom she'd been introduced to at a very young age! This was me and I needed this element in my life! But what body was this soul sitting in?

Ever since puberty hit, my body was strong. I was physically fit and I had energy without bounds. My weight was healthy; I was always around 52kgs. The world witnessed me as a bubbly and bright girl, who was on top of life. I was never classed as superficial or shallow. Did I love my reflection at this age? Had I ever loved my reflection, even before then? No. What I felt when I saw my reflection was far from love. But I believed this image staring back at me was the only thing I stood for and therefore I hated my whole self. But it was fine. I had no reason to ever feel anything else. I'd made peace with the fact that I wasn't beautiful or attractive. I was aware that life can be unfair and I knew I couldn't be greedy and have it all.

When I looked at my appearance and related this to my position within my family, the unfairness of life was confirmed. Each sibling had been given something special. I THOUGHT this to be true and therefore created this truth within my heart and so it would eventually become my own reality: sister number one was the dependable and wise voice; sister number two was the loving and sensitive heart; sister number four was the beauty and the attraction of the family and the only boy was the special one, for simple fact of being the only boy. But, hang on! What happened to sister number three? If I couldn't be the wise, the love, the beauty or the special one, I'd give myself a different label. Everyone within the family had their uniqueness and I could find my own. The reflection I saw at that age was going to start representing someone who was fit, strong, energized and healthy without bounds. I would be the crazy chick, the mad hatter and the one everyone wanted to befriend. In terms of relationships, I'd already proven myself to be unworthy of love, and again, I'd made peace with this unfair truth of divided worthiness within the world. And so the belief of 'never a beauty in the mirror, but always a queen of the party' is what I started making myself out to be. By starting the next chapter of my life, this label and I, soon would be a match made in heaven.

***

At this point, I had an aching heart for the loss of my first love—which took years to heal. I carried that pain safely with me, letting it go stale and sour, as I was strong and confident in the knowledge that I didn't deserve to be loved and felt no shame in admitting this 'truth'. So dealing with the emotions didn't feel to be necessary as I was happy to own them, deep down. The timing of this shattered heart was perfect, because only a month afterwards—which was also shortly after completing a three-year administrative college course that followed my high school years—I was moving to the city of Breda, to start my degree. This step led me away from one part of my reality and I started creating a new world with a new reality.

I chose to do a two-year course in tourism, specializing in tour-guiding. This was my desperate attempt to break away from a life in Holland that felt to be too structured and planned. I saw it as my ticket to freedom. And I'd surely never be classed as mundane by pursuing a dream of travel; being mundane was something I was almost too eager to avoid. This course in tourism was guiding me towards something I truly felt would bring my soul satisfaction and nourishment; it would fill the empty void. It was a decision based on what I'd always valued and what I'd seen around me whilst growing up: to travel is to be free, creatively inspired and it also shows the world you're larger than life. That's all I wanted! I wanted to be larger than life itself. This was a vision I didn't feel was unattainable for someone so determined and motivated.

I knew, even at this young age, that my dream was to embrace the world, to touch the hearts of other people and to be the vibrant soul that could put smiles on the faces of others. Such a dream of simplicity! How innocently I wanted to give all of myself to everyone else. I thought, still ever so innocently, that this was normal and it's what all young people desired. I believed that being young and free was to hop, skip and jump around this wonderful earth, whilst laughing and smiling with all of the passion and strength a person can muster. I figured it's the intention of the young. But, if it was the intention of every youthful soul on earth, then I needed to push myself and excel at being better and faster at hopping, skipping and jumping around this amazing planet. That was the only way for me to leave my mark and to be unique.

I was starting to play the game of life, but deep down I was struggling between wanting to be loved for my achievements—which meant I'd have to be perfect and fit in—and being loved for being different—which meant I'd have to go against normality and stand out. To deal with this, I worked at creating something of a façade behind which I could hide the deep longing I had to feel special. I worked on forming the façade that consisted of smiles, laughter and drunken madness.

I excelled as a person but I didn't excel as a student. I wasn't top of the class nor was I ever encouraged by my teachers that I'd make it big in the world of tour-guiding. The façade meant I was viewed as being the class clown—the one to make everyone laugh, the one to be too wild and lacking in professionalism. What I'd set out to do was truly becoming my reality. I now WAS the mad hatter! The label I'd given myself, when taking my family into account, was now my reality. It was a reputation of individuality. I was finally able to put smiles on people's faces! My lifelong task was now being fulfilled and it was my constant source of worthiness. Maintenance was always of the essence and this meant I needed to constantly excel to keep the level of satisfaction I was experiencing, on the rise.

Such pride I felt for being known as the mad hatter. But I never truly questioned my reasons for feeling so accomplished for something that requires no personality whatsoever, something that anybody can achieve! I never properly reflected on my behaviour and I figured every student parties excessively. It's nothing out of the ordinary. I didn't feel there could have been something more going on, underneath.

Only once or twice did I, ever so briefly, question my urgency, especially when I compared my need for parties and alcohol, to that of my dear friends. They knew their limits, yet I never did. They didn't depend on it for fun, yet my party nights were incomplete without rolling home intoxicated. They didn't love the hangovers, yet for me the hangovers were welcomed. Hangovers were proof of having brought self-destruction into my life through consuming this ever dependable substance. As others grew out of the urgency to always long for an abundant flow of alcohol to be seeping through their bloodstream, I stuck to what I knew best and alcohol was my friend. I continued to live what I believed was a full and happy way of life.

On hindsight, as ever is the case, I can only conclude that there was indeed an extra force at work. And in my early twenties, what started out as a simple pursuit of pleasure, slowly evolved into something more. It was my unique way of showing everyone what I was capable of. Alcohol made me stand strong, I was on top of the world and it brought the 'desire of the youth' to life. It urged me along and it was a substance I could never get enough of.

I completed the course successfully, with extreme effort. I struggled, but I made it and I proved to those who didn't believe in me, that they were so wrong! I'd done what I initially had set out to do and achieved something amazing on many different levels. I was standing out of the crowd and I had a university degree in my pocket! The field in which I'd achieved such brilliance, being travel, meant I was showing the world, as well as myself, that I was ready to truly start leaving my mark on this amazing planet.

 **4**

MAY 2004

With my diploma being my ticket to freedom, alcohol and I were
ready to rock the world from 2004 onwards. I was so capable of
indulging in this substance. It would stand in my favour, it was
always and everywhere so accessible and it would constantly show
just how tough and strong I was. The manner I chose in which to
give life to my dreams and to express my self, was nothing to be
considered soulful. Yet, I felt strongly that this was my purpose
and there simply couldn't be anything else in life that would make
me happier than travelling and partying. I was taking alcohol with
me along the road I was destined to follow and I was becoming the
'queen of the dance floor' wherever I touched ground.

Venturing to London in the summer of 2004 was my first big
step towards a life where work and travel were combined. It was
a new beginning and it felt it to be the start of bigger things. I'd
come so far, by the age of twenty-one, all by myself and I knew
I could make it even further. And I did. In August I returned
to Holland, and after three months of reluctantly pausing and
living a Dutch life, I needed to continue increasing my level
of independency through travel. So I hit the Austrian Alps in
December of 2004, for four months, to work on a ski resort as a
receptionist. I then found myself to be on a roll, so I flew to Greece
in April of 2005, where I worked in a hotel for six months.

The friend who was travelling with me never left my side
throughout these adventures and during these first eighteen

months after leaving college, I became more motivated to rock the world with my extreme drinking behaviour. The jobs I was working in and the surroundings in which they took place were focused on one thing: party life. I'd consciously placed myself in such environments, knowing what opportunities could come my way. I wasn't intending on using these opportunities to climb the career ladder. My target was different. I was pursuing the goal of self-destruction in order to do myself and my country of origin so proud!

***

I was now travelling and tourism was my branch. To state that tourism is solely focused on parties and boozing, isn't the reality. However, for me, at that point in time, it was. Throughout college I'd been discouraged by teachers when I'd express an interest in specializing in coach tour-guiding. I'd proven to everybody, including myself, to possess nothing of the expertise or professionalism that's required when working with tourists who want to touch base with the culture, heritage, history and authentic lifestyles that organized coach trips can offer. I was the party animal after all! With this discouragement, I figured I was only fit to work with tourists who were on a party mission. The requirements of the coach tour guides were measurements I'd never reach, but those of the holiday reps were in alignment with the reputation I'd worked so hard to achieve. So I surrounded myself with young party tourists for nearly eighteen solid months and it felt to be the best thing for me to do!

Amazing times is mostly what I can remember. When I say 'mostly', it's not because the times I don't take into account were less than amazing, but it's because they were simply hazy and forgotten, due to the presence of my dear friend. Alcohol and I welcomed many incidents that in actuality should've been a wake-up call telling me I was pushing myself to my drinking limits. The experiences that accompanied this party lifestyle were more than likely telling me to get my act into gear and to lay off excessive drinking. But I ignored every call and every sign. I was never fazed by incidents that occurred. I didn't flinch when waking-up beside strange men in houses I hadn't a notion of their geographical location, all for lack of self-respect. I wasn't bedazzled when falling asleep on the dance floor yet still being able to stand strong, feel the vibes of the music and dance my heart out, all for not wanting to admit defeat. Even when falling asleep on the ice and having a layer of snow as my blanket in −15°C 'heat', I felt nothing close to the shock I should've felt, all for wanting to be the 'last man standing'. I didn't care that my daily routine revolved around the set-task of curing the looming hangover with junk food so as to start the vodka binge again at 6pm night after night, all for wanting to be strong. I thought life couldn't get any better. I didn't want to nor could I deny my well-developed talent of being able to drink ten beers each night and feel strangely fine, all for the lack of just about everything that can be associated with love for oneself.

These were my adventures. These were my stories. These, I felt at one stage, were what I lived for and what I needed to share with the world. I had to tell the tales of *'How I survived drunken incidents that could have potentially been life-threatening'*. So proud I was and these times were what I classed, for many years, as being the best years of my life.

To suddenly say they are no longer such treasures isn't true. These times, so hazy and insane, brought some amazingly special people into my life and they will always hold special places in my heart. This is one of the reasons why I treasure these memories. People make the places. People add to the experiences. People give you the connection. And that's something I've always believed

so strongly in. So I embarked on these journeys with a substance
I classed as a friend and each time, I returned with so many more.

***

This substance so potent was an important factor in my life.
I didn't care of the consequences this abuse was having on my
body. I didn't care that it was a big motivator in terms of decisions
I made in life. I seemed so full of the normal youngster madness
and I planned to continue along these lines. Alcohol was simply an
outlet for this urgency I had to push myself to self-destruction. This
drive was a representation of the lack of love I had for myself. If a
person doesn't love themselves, then how can they feel deserving of
the love that would be expressed in caring for oneself? Why would
they ever treat themselves kindly? Lack of love promotes self-harm.
And to suppress such a strong feeling of hatred towards oneself is
almost painful. For me, boozing not only numbed this feeling of
secret pain, unworthiness and self-hatred but it was upholding the
reputation I'd worked so hard on gaining, throughout the years.
For me, this was the perfect road to travel upon. I'd seen it in my
surroundings as a child and teenager, I knew of its strength. And
what started as my way to enjoy parties as a teenager had slowly
evolved into my way of opening up the door of unlimited potential,
hence the reason for me to have wanted parties and alcohol without
limits.

During those eighteen months of travel, I compared myself to
my friends, who were living somewhat of a more stable life back
in Holland. They were calming down. They were going through
that period of change that everybody goes through, usually within
a few years of leaving college: setting up an orderly, controlled
and structured life with everyday responsibilities and stabilities.
Maturity is what the majority in society will call this. I call this
an individual choice of living. I knew then that it wasn't for me.

It wasn't going to happen. I also couldn't understand how or why young adults would choose to go against something so brilliant that was on offer in world. That 'something' being: youth, travel and parties! I judged them and found their behaviour to be a sign of weakness; they were deserting the nightlife and the drinking sessions. I couldn't comprehend how they were able to feel happy! Likewise, there's not a doubt in my mind that they too judged me, for the actions I took. I thought their judgement was more an expression of jealously for the amazing life I was living and so I didn't let anybody slowdown the drive I'd been using when travelling and partying as much as I could.

With this, the pace at which I would live my life forever was fixed. On the odd occasion I'd take three seconds out of my life, to look at how I was living in that moment. All I could see was Niamh, trying to run around the world, party hard and live extremely. On these fleeting moments I wondered how I'd keep up the pace, as the visions alone of having such a future (which I figured was inevitable seeing as though this way of living was the only life that would bring me happiness), exhausted me. But I couldn't go against this energy and this race, so I let those moments fly and continued to stay high on the experiences of travel.

***

The race that had become my life, started when I left college. This race only had one competitor, which was me. But it felt as though there were so many others. Billions! Six billion to be precise! I was competing AGAINST the whole world and the racetrack was taking me AROUND the world, all at the same time. Like magic!

On the occasions when I dropped out I experienced the extreme opposite of 'extended periods of ultimate highs'. During these periods, the ground was suddenly too close for comfort, the high-flying chapters had been closed, I was mundane and my life felt to be in ruins. I'd come to value travel so much and I couldn't believe there to be any other way I could live and be happy—so I figured it best to crumble. The first period of dropping out of the race happened after returning from London. I stayed in Holland for three months and the second period came after my Greek adventure, which brought me to Ireland for ten long months.

When I wasn't participating in the race, it was always still ongoing. In my mind I was still racing and so were the billions of others—yet they were moving and I wasn't! The reality wasn't reflecting the visions I was holding on to so strongly, so there was a collision and the world around me wasn't coinciding with the purpose I felt to have in this life. My life was failing to represent what my heart and mind needed to experience. So of course I felt like a failure. I had no sense of purpose and feelings of heartache were mine. This heartache never discouraged me nor did it make me less of a believer. It only strengthened the feeling that the world and I, we needed to experience each other so badly! And my lists and lists of places I needed to go and of experiences I needed to have, were proof of my excitement for life. I held the vision of the world and the world held a vision of me (I hoped!).

Whether or not I was flying high in the sky or on the ground trying to take-off, I was unaware that I needed travel to express my inner desires. I was unaware why dropping out of the race felt so bad. The heartache and loss I felt on the ground, never made me question the truth behind my urgency to fly. I never related creativity to travel. I've since realized that by temporarily not travelling, there was no creative life being lived, nothing of ME was being shared and it was a minor suppression of my need for expression. So I was secretly burdening my soul.

I wanted an extraordinary life and believed it was the only thing that would bring me happiness. But to keep feeling that same level of happiness I needed more and more and so I always had to keep on pushing. I was constantly trying to break down the gates that were standing between the 'normality' of society and the 'difference' I wanted to experience. That's where I believed my happiness was to be found.

5

OCTOBER 2005

By 2005, at the age of twenty-two, my appearance and weight had gone through different changes. Before I started my travels, I'd maintained the healthy weight of 52kgs. I wasn't obsessed with this number, nor would I weigh myself frequently. I looked and felt physically strong. I had phases of going to the gym or taking fitness classes. I always tried to be healthy and be the representation of the label I'd applied as a teenager (fit and healthy daughter number three).

Once I started travelling, first to London and later Austria, drinking gallons of alcohol and eating mountains of junk food took its toll on my physical body and I was no longer the healthy 52kgs. Throughout this period I'd given up any desire I had to be healthy. The toned figure that I'd always claimed was ME had disappeared beneath 4kgs of fat produced from beer. My face was the bearer of this extra weight—and it was weight that felt to be of the world! My head had almost exploded and my nose had spread across my already ugly face. But happy is how I felt. On the surface, it was a dead set. Remarks were flying around my ears stating how healthy I looked—when really what people meant to say was that I'd gained too much weight. But I'd brush the actual meaning of these remarks to one side. Because I'd been living an amazing life so far! Paying the high price of a healthy body wasn't too high—not with the adventures I'd experienced and the stories I was able to tell. The experiences were far more fulfilling than anything my weight might project. But really, with my short height of 1.54cm, my weight felt to be excessive. When the scales showed 56kgs I found it was time for me to get back into shape!

Only six months later, by October 2005, I was in the best shape of my life. Yes! I was so strong, toned and full of proper health! I'd been working in Greece for six months as an activity and fitness instructor. So my physical body had benefitted without a doubt. I was the representation of full life! I was glowing and had achieved this figure in only six months! This was something so many others would be envious of! The scales, once again, showed 52kgs. But these 52kgs were of real substance. I felt to be a better ME, I was high quality and finally living up to the label I'd secretly given myself. Life was suddenly amazing. At that point in time, I wasn't only travelling and being the big drinker, the 'queen of parties' and living a life that wasn't mundane, but I was also fitting the perfect description of health!

From then onwards an inner strength had been realized. I discovered something more I was capable of achieving. It felt amazing to have become so healthy within six short months. The complements I received from others, stating how well I looked, added to my feeling of accomplishment. The outside world was suddenly speaking words that were filling my heart with the uniqueness I believed I was. It was all the confirmation I needed of the 'truth' that happiness is found in the outside world. And so, just like many others, I was a true believer that happiness lies in the things we see and experience and also in the recognition and complements we receive from others. 'What I see, is my happiness. I see a healthy girl. What I do, is my happiness. I party and I travel. What I consume, is my happiness. I drink alcohol and I now eat healthy'. I'd mentally landed myself in a place where my determination, strength, passion and drive would truly serve a purpose.

I state that I'd found this lifestyle satisfying me. But really I was by no means feeling fulfilled. I knew of the opportunities within the world and the potential of what I could become and what I was capable of. There were no limits. If I knew this and if I felt with all my heart that I was capable of grasping every opportunity life presents us with, then how would I ever feel satisfied with what I was doing and where I was going? There was always more! And without having more, I felt to be less. And to feel less was painful, so I aimed to reach those non-existing limits and I pushed myself continuously. I had to reach higher and higher, just to feel the same level of satisfaction. My life was for the purpose of reaching those ends that were nowhere. And for as long as the world was turning and I was still breathing, I could do nothing other than push and stretch myself always.

The second occasion I dropped out of the race was from October 2005. I was 'forced' to stay in Ireland for ten long months, by issues I felt to have no control over. I say this, but it was my own choice to return to Ireland. I'd given myself the new task of working harder than ever before in the field of tourism that wasn't suiting my college reputation of being the class clown. I was taking to coach tour-guiding! This meant I was going to prove to the world (or to the teachers at the university—even if I had no contact with them whatsoever) that they were ALL wrong and that I was capable of being the professional and confident guide. Another achievement to put on my list that would eventually add-up to the sum total of happiness! Also this new job would provide the much needed funds so as to travel to Australia. This was the new goal I had in sight: reaching that amazing country by September 2006.

***

During the months of preparing for Australia, I wasn't in the position of being the party animal nor was I travelling far and wide. I felt as if I was abandoning two parts of me because of this. For this reason, I subconsciously figured what I needed to do was to sustain the reflection I saw in the mirror. It represented a happy, healthy and beautiful façade to the world. I was losing the party façade throughout this long period so I had to cling to something else. I started making the shift from one form of concealment—being parties and alcohol—to a different form—being my appearance. This added purpose to my life, my life that suddenly had become sour for lack of movement in space as I found myself to be stationary, regardless of the fact that my mind was still running.

My purpose was starting to show! During the ten months of being stuck in Ireland my weight dropped to 48kgs and because of this, my reflection was beautiful. It was even better than the reflection I had a year before. I was truly amazed by how good I felt to have lost a few kilos, all by learning to value a certain way of living—a way I'd never before experienced. Ten long months may have been torture in terms of 'abandoning my dreams'. But if my new weight was the result of this torture then it was worth its weight in gold, or worth its weight in 48kgs of whole entire self!

I'd stopped drinking and partying and, even in my sense of loss, my body felt amazing. No alcohol meant a massive decline in calorie intake. Usually I'd consume approximately 5000 calories through alcohol alone, each week. My body had been missing those empty calories, so this restriction definitely played a part when creating the image I saw in the mirror. As well it was a big contributor to my new feelings of fulfilment that accompanied my reflection.

The conscious application of a subtle change in my lifestyle led me to value my reflection, my weight and my feelings towards food, so much more. Life was so much better, as health was more important than binging on alcohol and fitness more important than dancing the night away. Throughout this period in Ireland, I'd taken to eating disciplined. Three healthy meals were enough to sustain myself. Fattening foods were banned, chocolate was an occasional and rare treat and snacking was a thing of the past. Exercise was something I devoted time to, be it walking or jogging or using the fitness equipment at home. I could feel so many benefits and it was amazing. And, with this sense of achievement, my time finally came. I was packing my backpack and heading to Australia! It was September 30th of 2006 and my goal had been reached!

 **6**

SEPTEMBER 2006

The adventure of a lifetime was about to commence: a year backpacking throughout Australia. It began in such a manner that I was sprinting. I felt that by running towards a dream, I'd make it my reality sooner rather than later. In my haste I'd brought many extra 'things' along with me. This wasn't my initial intention, but these 'things' had become a part of me and would make my adventure into the rollercoaster ride it was meant to be.

What had I taken with me, as I boarded the plane? First off, I'd taken the words that had been spoken to me, by friends and family. They were words representing the voices of the whole world, and they stated, 'Niamh, you're looking amazing!', 'Niamh, you can say goodbye to that new figure of yours, once you get to Australia!', 'Niamh, the alcohol and unhealthy living you'll be doing, just like every other traveller, will make you so big!', 'Niamh, you're going to return from Australia looking like you did when you returned from Austria, being 56kgs!' Such a heavy load I was carrying. Adding to the weight, I was carrying pictures of the "exploded" head I'd returned with from Austria one-and-a-half years previous (The head that was being carried by a body that was intoxicated with alcohol). These pictures were just subtle reminders of what results I'd create if I took to excessive drinking again. The fear of becoming what those voices of the world were expecting of me suddenly wasn't the only fear. As I flew myself away from normality and towards a free dream, I feared that once

I'd touch base with the kangaroos, didgeridoos, boomerangs and BBQs, I'd feel that this particular goal would be the ultimate peak of achievement in my life and there'd be nothing left for me to work towards. I didn't know how I could possibly allow myself to live and enjoy the desired freedom without having anything else to cling to. How could I let myself GO and embrace the once-in-a-lifetime experience I'd worked so hard to achieve, if I didn't have anything else going for me?

The final 'thing' I was carrying, was the uncontrollable urge to make-up for lost time after being deprived of binge drinking and parties for ten months. Suddenly being the person who was able to rock around the world, meant I'd be living my dream. But such a lifestyle was sure to take its toll on my new found weight, reflection, figure and feelings of worthiness! How was I going to uphold the reputation of being the party animal once again, when my healthy weight—which I'd gradually come to value MORE— wouldn't be sustained by my past desires to indulge in my so-called best friend? Was my year in Australia going to work out, if I continued to live according to my newly acquired values? How would I cope with travelling in such fear?

With red desert plains appearing before me, achievements were slowly starting to vanish. So setting a new goal was the only thing I could do to make my year of travelling somewhat bearable. It would've otherwise been torture for a non-deserving and unworthy soul who was incapable of loving herself, to have simply let go and endured such brilliance.

The new target I was aiming for, even though I didn't have a clue of the true issues behind my new purpose and goal, was very much in accordance with the voices of the world that were ringing in my ear. My target was matching my reasons for taking the pictures of my once exploded face with me as I ventured and my aim would sustain the number of my weight and would give me more ease when curing the craving for alcohol. My new goal was in perfect harmony with the longing I had for my reflection to send out positive vibes that were only truly felt if I was proving to everyone at home that I was different than other backpackers in Australia. My target was simple: I was going to return to Ireland one year later, and not have gained an ounce of weight! This was easy, I could do this and it gave my adventure the extra purpose it needed. All I wanted was to prove the voices of the world wrong. That's just a small dream to pursue, compared to the dream of travelling Australia! And I could make this all possible by drinking to excess, by restricting my food intake, by partying like never before and by receiving all the necessary vitamins from the sun. Life would be amazing!

The goal I'd set was the reason for my actions. My actions were the reasons for my smiles, my energy, my positive vibes and my confidence. The deeper meaning behind the actions was never clear. They were buried, they were unseen and they were unknown. And so I never considered anything to be destructive. I had my healthy priorities, and that was it!

***

On first arriving, I already had most of the discipline set up in my daily life. So working towards this new achievement, wasn't all that big of a deal. All I needed was some extra strength, some stricter rules and more awareness as to what I was putting in my body. I decided I would create a balance between the alcohol I consumed, the food I reluctantly ate and the amount of exercise I did. Starting from the moment I entered Oz.

Throughout the first ten days, the people who came into my life were amazing. The drinking sessions I had were second to none. I woke up everyday smiling to the world, just for the fact that I was Down Under. I felt I'd found my place of comfort, fulfilment and adventure, especially with the new set of rules by which I started to live. My travel buddies all planned their trip through Oz, focusing on the must-sees and must-dos of Australia. Every traveller I came across seemed to own one of these lists, be it in their journal, or in their minds. This was probably the reason for me to have NOT travelled in such a manner. I had other things in mind. I'd created a vision of travelling through Australia, using my new values of restriction as the drive upon which I would thrive. The other important motivator I used was the simple fact that I needed to financially support my travels. So I chose to work wherever I went. I found more importance in actually doing something productive, rather than taking excursions, hanging out in hostels, going to the pubs and lying under the hot Australian sun. I figured it was my personal adventure, it was my dusty desert road upon which I was tripping and I chose to let it take me wherever the work was, regardless of what others were doing. And so, after the first ten days, I set off by myself, in search of work, in search of a different Australia.

I moved to the middle of nowhere, to a town that felt to be the set of an American Country & Western movie, from a time way before any of the current residents were born. I couldn't believe how lucky I was to be on such an adventure. But no matter how amazing everything felt to be and no matter how big the distractions around me were, I never forgot my rules. Throughout the days before arriving in the Wild West I was thinking along the extreme lines of not needing food if I wasn't physically active. I was actually living accordingly. I was trying to starve myself. It was working! But the step into the Wild West, which was in aid of finding a fruit picking job, stopped me from depriving myself so extremely. I had to sacrifice those amazing feelings I'd get when giving power to this inner voice that was starting to speak to me, saying I didn't need food.

The hard work on the farm commenced, my eating resumed and life felt to be so unfair! Because I knew I had the ability to stop eating and I knew I had the strength to live on next to nothing and party as much as I wanted. But working in the hot Australian 40°C heat for eight hours a day, meant an extra source of energy was required, even if there was an extra force at work within.

In order to let myself eat, I had to push myself in other ways, just to create that much needed balance. For two months, I was ecstatic for what I was creating and for how I was living. Each day I ate according to strict rules. No fat, no grease, no snacks, no treats. No eating after 8pm. I would eat small amounts every four hours and the main foods were fruit, cereals, yoghurts, fish, rice and noodles. Protein and carbohydrates weren't allowed to be eaten in the same meal. Alcohol was without limits, as long as I was sticking to these eating patterns. The harder I worked, the more alcohol I deserved. If I ever ate more than my unwritten rules, I would need to work harder. On the weekends, I would go running in 40°C heat, through the red dirt, with the sun beating down on my hatless head. But this was good because it meant I was allowed to drink more beer in the afternoon. Fellow travellers living in the same hostel were only persuading me to keep up this healthy way of living. They said how impressed they were, how strong I was and what a great figure I had.

This two-month period I always considered as being one of the best of my year. I met some of the most special people, who have supported me from afar throughout my toughest times. This period also gave me the true Australian experience I longed to have as well as setting my rules firmly in place and making me feel worthy of fully engaging in the amazing life that was broadening my horizons through travels. I was such a happy person and for this reason, I never questioned why I was choosing to live my dream in such a manner. I simply headed to the next place, carrying my heavy backpack loaded with my passion for life and rules of restrictions.

***

At the start of the new year magical New Zealand was welcoming me and another extremely special lady for a month. Kelly and I met each other during our first days in Oz and we felt such a strong connection that we wanted to travel more together. We opted for the land of kiwis and we set the dates by which we would leave Australia, within the first days of meeting each other. The farm work was in aid of this trip and so, once the dollars were in, we were out of Oz! Our excitement was contagious. We were both in such a hurry to get to New Zealand to do some proper backpacking. But we actually forgot to stop running once we were there! I personally never properly absorbed what New Zealand had to offer. I was way too eager to continue the race and couldn't wait to get to Australia so as to find more farming work. As beautiful as New Zealand is, I didn't fully appreciate my time there. On hindsight I can see why. It was due to temporarily having nothing to drive me, nothing to cling to. It was pure vacating and that was considered as a burden and it felt like punishment. The only thing that was driving me through New Zealand was the potential of what Australia could offer me, in terms of living a balanced travel and working lifestyle.

Stepping foot once again on Australian soil at the beginning of February, was the relief I needed. I was back in the race and in search of work. One of the biggest triumphs of my whole year in Australia was experienced, when I managed to land myself a job as a rockmelon picker. I still had Kelly by my side up until the moment I was sure the job was mine. It was actually through her guidance and help that I was back in the race. There were unforeseen circumstances and minor obstacles that we both saw as opportunities and so embraced the adventure of *'getting Niamh a farming job'* with as much passion as we could muster. And what an accomplished couple we both felt to be! Within a week of arriving back in Oz, I was full of the joys of life as I sweltered in the 44°C heat, picking melons from the ground and continuously marching at least ten miles a day, behind an ever-moving tractor.

This was a six-week experience of lifetime once again, mainly because of the fact that just about every aspect of this work and live-in situation would've been considered as punishment to those who feel worthy of all the goodness on the planet. Because honestly, there's little pleasure to be experienced when living in a garage, sharing a room with ten others, sleeping on urine-stained mattresses, having mice visiting on a regular basis and being unable to casually leave the farm for living so isolated. Torture for most, heaven for me! I must admit that on the first day I wondered if prisoners in jail cells lived under better circumstances. The second day I woke up and truly felt to be living in hell and the third day I woke up and was happy to endure. The application of my strict behaviour made it even more pleasurable. So I was in hell and heaven, all at once.

To add to my heaven, I continued to restrict in terms of food and I pushed myself during the hours of picking. Alcohol was taking on a slightly different role at this stage. I was starting to worry more about the calories that alcohol would give me rather than about what others would think of me when NOT choosing to drink vast amounts. I gained extra strength by applying some rules regarding my alcohol consumption. It was no longer as much and as often as possible, but now it was only on certain nights and no more than a set amount.

***

I'd been in Australia for six months by March 2007. I hadn't been weighing myself nor had I seen myself in a full length mirror. The weighing scales was a scarce thing to come by, when living on farms, just as the mirror was. But I did manage on one particular day to find a place where I'd be able to check if my good behaviour had been paying off or not. I was getting desperate to find out if the number on the scales was going to bring uncountable feelings of fear to my mind (if I'd gained weight over the past six months) or if it would bring just one lonely feeling of love to my heart (if I'd remained the same weight).

So whilst finally standing in front of the mirror I was delighted by what I saw. My reflection after six months excelled every other reflection I'd ever witnessed of myself, at any other point in my entire life, in terms of perfection. I was feeling stronger for the physical work I'd been undergoing and it showed! My muscles were defined because the layer of fat was less. Fat was no longer hiding this treasured strength. My clothes were baggy and it felt so good. My face was smaller too, so this was definitely making my goal of 'not having an exploded head when returning to Ireland' a reality. All the good behaviour I'd been applying during the first half of my year, was working a treat. That word 'treat'! It was becoming a word to make my mouth water. But my reflection urged my taste buds to turn off to their ever-increasing need for something containing fat and sugars. Standing on the scales only strengthened my mind to turn off any feelings of needing more food. On that same day, the scales showed 45kgs. Again, feelings of delight filled my stomach. I hadn't a clue how I'd made that come about. I'd lost 4kgs within six months! The freaky thing about this new piece of information was that I hadn't really been aiming to LOOSE those 4kgs. All I wanted was to NOT gain the weight I'd lost throughout the months I spent in Ireland! I figured though, if being 45kgs made me feel this good then I'd aim to STAY this weight.

***

By April I already had two work experiences under my belt—the one that needed more and more holes so as to uphold my jeans.

I was on a mission to have an experience of a different kind. The farms had been amazing and now I wanted to work in an outback country pub. This I figured would be a challenge. I would be faced with alcohol being served in extreme measures. I wasn't sure how I'd cope with the inconvenient possibility of gaining the weight I had so gradually lost up until that point in time. I'd be challenging my new values and it was a risk. I felt threatened as I could see there was a likelihood of my ultimate goal fading into the distance. This prospect darkened my mind. Risk and fear go hand in hand and I was driven by both. I was a courageous adult and I needed to test my strengths. After all, that's all I was living for.

A week after leaving the melon farm, I arrived at my new location. It was my new place of heaven and my new place of hell, all within the walls of the pub where I'd be living and working as the only barmaid. I was the only backpacker, the only outsider. I was surrounding myself with alcohol and for six days a week I was getting paid to serve what I once had considered to be my best friend. I was feeding the local community their own personal poison and it felt like both a sinful pleasure and sweet punishment all at once. It was a pleasure because I knew I was the passage through which they received their source of happiness—what a gift I'd been given! It was a pleasure because the perks of the job were letting me indulge in that same substance, night after night, just like the locals. It was punishment because I wanted to reject what these perks would do to my body, but I simply couldn't resist, for fear of losing the reputation of being the 'queen of the party'.

Was alcohol still my best friend or had it become my enemy? It was both. This three-month period revolved around that so-called friend, whether we were on good terms or bad. It didn't matter if I was putting my goal on the line and taking risks by being in pub. There was no time to reflect. This was life after all and life was still a race—the race that was against the six billion other people in the world that was taking me around the world, simultaneously. In addition to this race I was running, life had also become a competition, a competition between the goodness I was seeing in the mirror and the temptation of food. In order to win I had to use my secret weapon of strength that I held on to deep down. It permitted me to fight against myself, so bravely.

I saw in my surroundings many different methods of destruction I could use to my advantage. In every which way I could, I used my environment to aid the sustenance of the already created perfection I saw in the mirror. The food restrictions that had been applied so far were no longer enough. They needed to be tighter. I started to eat less by combining breakfast and lunch. Meaning I was eating two meals a day. Brunch was a bowl of cornflakes and dinner was either a form of protein and vegetables or a toasted sandwich with extra cereal to fill me up. These restrictions were in addition to my visits to the local gym. I would go three times a week in the morning time and I'd make an extra effort when a hangover would be lurking outside my bedroom door, which was four mornings a week. Occasionally I would take to running around the very small town and I also introduced myself to yoga by borrowing a book from the library and making it my mission to become a self-taught professional. The amazing poses offered me flexibility and an evermore toned physic. The deeper meaning of yoga wasn't important to me. I had my priorities in order, and lean is what I desired to be! I also started to use the people around me as extra motivators. Whenever friends would indulge in unhealthy food, I would gain strength to resist. Whenever they would joke that my drinking would soon be the reason for weight gain, I would aim to tighten the belt a little more. Everything and everyone around me, was working in perfect order. Balance is what I'd created during those three months of bliss!

 **7**

JULY 2007

The pinnacle of Australia is where Darwin lies. It's also where I found the pinnacle of my trip, in terms of how I needed to excel when reaching the ultimate goal of returning home without extra weight. In this isolated yet thriving town, skills and expertise of a different league were needed to be called upon. This ten-week period turned out to be the final port of call before my return home. I'd been running around Australia for nine months, by that stage, without realizing that with every mile I ran, the clock was also ticking at an ever-increasing pace. My goal was approaching at high speed. And as with any goal in life, running towards it, lets us fully appreciate our triumph and relish in our glory. I was saving the best for last. The energy for the sprint would come out of nowhere, just when I needed it most.

The first two weeks were torture. I witnessed myself becoming the typical traveller. I was suddenly treating my adventure as being an extended booze fest in the sun. This was only the second time since the start of my trip, to be continuously faced with enjoyment to such an extent. So I knew that choosing for this location to be the one where I would have my last Australian adventure through work and play, I had my work cut out.

The first two weeks I partied and drank excessively, night after night. I spent every cent I owned and I binged on fatty takeaways after every drinking session. I was bringing myself to destruction. My health was deteriorating and I felt I was getting fat for indulging in both food and alcohol, but how I enjoyed the parties!

How I loved to dance, how I loved to rule the floor, how I loved to leave my mark and become known as the mad soul of the night. Such goodness felt like so much torture. I was again in heaven and hell. It was fulfilling and overbearing. It was soothing and painful. It was bright and dark. Pleasures no longer felt like pleasures, the parties felt like sins, the drinking felt like poison and the sun felt to be burning every last ounce of self-respect I had, leaving only ashes to take up that spot which had never been large to begin with.

I was letting myself experience as much pleasure as my body could take. But what was it that I now classed as pleasure? What did I class as endurance? I couldn't distinguish the difference anymore. Was it pleasurable to feel the rays of sun, to experience the weeks of parties, to socialize with travellers and to feel in a relaxed holiday-mode? Surely I was enduring!

Without self-respect I felt punishment was the pleasure I should have been indulging in. It was the best I felt life had to offer me and I had to take it. During the first two weeks in Darwin, I wasn't. I was off-course for a short period of time. I'd been led astray and only had myself to blame and when blame is placed, the one who is the bearer, needs to suffer.

***

After two weeks of neglecting the proper pleasures, I had a high price to pay. An out-of-body experience followed. And when looking back and witnessing myself as I sat on the floor of the hostel dorm, this is what I see.

She's in tears and doesn't know why. She's speaking to a special friend. She's opening-up and telling her how much of a waste of space she is. She claims to have wasted nine precious months of her life, by travelling around Australia achieving absolutely nothing. She's literally out of her mind with grief for what she's done. But what exactly she has DONE, she can only state as being

NOTHING. Nothing good, nothing bad, nothing ventured, nothing gained, nothing achieved, nothing attained. What a waste of a life. But she still has more than two months to go before the race around Australia is over. She knows she will only be the winner if she can run towards her goal. How will she keep up in the race if she's sitting on the floor of the dorm? How can she pick herself back up off the ground and face the world, when she hasn't got an ounce of love in her heart? She even spoke words she thought would never pass her lips, 'If a ticket to Ireland comes falling out of the sky, I'll be on a plane in a flash!' But when speaking these words, suddenly there's something else.

There's a strength that was picking her up. It was a strength that would give her the love she needed. It wasn't her friend that was sleeping on the bunk bed below or the friend she was talking so intensely to. Instead it was a friend who had slowly made her presence felt over the past year. This lost girl had no clue of the danger that came when grasping that invisible hand. She had no clue whom this hand belonged to nor what her motives, her origins or her goals were. Had she rejected this strong hand, this crumbled girl—lost in her depression—would have boarded a plane back to where she came from, where she knew there was a source of love, something she was no longer capable of providing for herself.

Blinded by the clouds that weren't to be seen in the bright blue Australian sky, she grabbed the strong hand of the only one who would help her win the race and win the competition against her reflection. Had there been words written in the clouds that were invisibly hanging above her head, then this is what would have been seen, 'Two more months Niamh, you've come so far. You will fail by not lifting yourself up off the ground. So it's simply not an option to give in. You have this extra strength now and you know what you must do. You can achieve anything.' She takes her hand,

*she wipes away her own tears, tells herself she is weak for feeling
so lost and depressed and gets on with life.*

This was a day I'll never forget and a scene that will never leave
my mind. It's where anorexia truly appeared as if out of magic.
Like a spell had been cast over me, the witch I shall refer to by
the name of Anna, was now in my life. I had no clue she was the
one whose hand I was taking, as being spellbound is always to the
oblivion of the one over whom the spell has been cast. With an
inability to see and an ignorance to know, the path was taking the
course it was meant to.

***

With my blurred vision, I was guided by someone I couldn't
see. I literally pulled myself up from the floor and walked into
an Italian restaurant, not in search of food or wine or any of
the other goodness that Italian fine dining has to offer. Instead
I was in search of a job. And ten minutes later, I walked out with
a waitressing position! This small simple step was such a big
achievement! I went from sitting on the floor in tears to having
a job, a goal and a new lease of life, within only a few hours!
Whoever it was that cast a spell over me, was truly a magical
being, if these were the results that could be achieved by following
that guidance!

Everything became clear from then onwards. Every other factor
of my so far wasted life suddenly fell into perfect accordance with
the rules I was told to tighten, by the same strength that helped me
stand up off the hostel floor. Waitressing wasn't a job I'd done in
the past, so I embraced the new experience by aiming to succeed
at being the fastest and the best—at all costs. The inner strength
was becoming more and more powerful and had to be obeyed in
order to keep my face smiling, my head clear, my body toned, my
legs running and my weight down. The power was being applied
in absolutely every aspect of my amazing life and this particular

job stimulated me from day one to push myself more than ever before. How? I had the opportunity to work everyday, if the owner so desired. I didn't let myself eat on-the-job. I forced myself to run around the restaurant instead of elegantly gliding through the labyrinth of tables. I happily drank only two mugs of coffee and classed these as my meals and I felt that a five-minute break was sufficient when working ten-hour shifts. This was only in terms of my working life. Did I have another life?

There was the unavoidable party scene I was reluctantly surrounded by, as I was living in a hostel with backpackers who only had one priority throughout their stay in Darwin: to party. The party life somehow seemed to gel with my working life. If I wasn't doing one, I was doing the other. Sleep wasn't too important, nor was food. Not when goals were being aimed for and reputations needed sustenance. Each day I was eating two meals consisting of fruit, muesli and yoghurt and a few times a week I'd happily eat vegetables, noodles or rice. Every night, the restaurant doors were closed and the focus of restrictions shifted from food to alcohol. Days were focused on counting calories, the litres of green tea I drank and the hours I ran without stopping or standing still. Nights were focused on drinking stronger substances than beer, containing as little volume as possible and with next to no calories but still acquiring the same or, preferably, higher results of drunkenness. The gelled and muddled days and nights were lived so as to balance the pleasures I wasn't worthy of experiencing and the pain I was meant to endure.

Changing my approach towards HOW and WHAT I was drinking was for the fact that I knew I was well able to drink large volumes. I'd had years of training when I was working on my reputation of forever being the 'queen of the parties'. But in Darwin, my previous reputation wasn't working in my favour. I wanted to be drunk all the time. But I wasn't happy to have to put so many empty calories in my toned body, in order to reach my desired level of drunkenness. So I consciously took to drinking either straight whiskey or vodka mixed with orange juice. The vodka mix was like a magic potion. It provided me with pleasure and drunkenness as well as the vitamins and minerals I was lacking. I knew I'd found the quickest and most efficient way to stay 'the queen of the parties' as well as the healthy traveller in a toned body (which I hoped others were envious of). I felt to be in a much safer place regarding my alcohol consumption, my food intake, my health, my body, my whole life.

So the reason for the smells of the Italian cuisine to have come my way, were so much deeper than I imagined. The aromas felt to be far more rewarding and fulfilling than actually eating the 14" pizza I would drool over throughout the hours of serving unhealthy food in the restaurant.

With the energy I was now receiving from this amazing lifestyle and this precious job, I knew I could live amazingly. The ultimate goal of 'not gaining weight' would be achieved, it was a dead set that I would win, especially with my extra guidance. I could see the finish line but wanted to be running faster so my victory would blow me away! I needed extra spice in my life; there wasn't yet enough. And so I decided to set the goal of travelling to Singapore, Malaysia and Thailand for a month before flying back home. This was an extra purpose to my existence. I was filling my ever-growing hunger because it was yet another way in which to restrict. As with every goal, something needs to be sacrificed. What I now had to give up was having money to spend. I had work every hour I could and save every hard earned cent in order to get to Asia for a month. Having applied food restrictions was actually a blessing in disguise; when there's no need to eat, there's no need to purchase. This was the spice I felt I was worthy of, because any other form of spice I definitely wasn't.

***

The spice of life. I wasn't allowed any of it. So needless to say that when I was faced with the potential of some romantic spice, rules needed to be tightened once again. A handsome new Italian bartender entered the restaurant. He had little English, yet was so determined to learn the language all on his own accord. The barrier of the language made the connection we developed, all the more special. It's not everyday you form an instant bond with someone, when the level of conversation is minimal. It's a rarity and with every rarity there is a speciality. The two of us clearly had something special. However 'best buddies' is what I called our connection. This was all I deserved. Actually, it was probably more than I deserved! Such love came from him and it was almost too much. It felt overwhelming to be so close to someone so treasured. However, I felt safe and protected to only see and relate to him as my best buddy. It was a restriction and it felt good. Secretly I soared on the feelings of energy I received when I was with him. I flew to higher plains. I adored him. I cherished our time together but never showed any of this.

Instead, I welcomed into my party nights an encounter with someone from a different European country: France. I never got very intimate with him, but he showed me that I was worthy of attention. In our moments of being together, I gave what I felt I was, which was NOTHING. Feelings of friendship were what I had towards him, even though we appeared to be more than just friends, to those around us. To me it was a way to distract myself from the amazement I was tempted by, when being around my best buddy. It meant I wasn't burdening the tall, dark and handsome Italian with only a fraction of the love he deserved to receive from a girl. My actions reflected what I felt I deserved at that point in time, which was clearly NOTHING.

But somebody must have received something of what I was offering to my surrounding world. Who was it? Who did I devote my time passionately to? The main man who received all of what I felt to be, was my boss. An Italian man who saw his waitresses as 'scrubbers', who pushed us all to our limits, who never gave us any recognition for who we were or for what we did. He was someone who was never satisfied no matter how fast we ran or how many hours we worked. We were being policed on the job at every single moment. He was dominant and powerful. He became the representation of inner strength I was embracing in my life, at that moment in time. That destructive voice inside myself adored this destructive physical presence outside myself. I gave to him all that I was. I gave to him my passion to succeed, to achieve and to prove. I gave to him my subconscious desire to harm myself, all so I could feel worthy of love. I had to run faster, work harder and eat less just to get his approval. Just like I had to run faster, work harder and eat less to get my own approval, but the approval, praise or recognition never came. It never came from him or me. It was perfect however, because his force strengthened my power and offered reassurance that my goal was being achieved. The child within was picking up on the similarities between the masculine energies I'd been influenced by as a young teenager, in the presence of my strong, dominant and powerful step-dad. Subconsciously I had my priorities in order. So I can only conclude that having fun with someone of French descent was just to show to myself and the world that I was somehow worthy of attention from a male; embracing an Italian man who I adored was a dream never to be realized; using my work environment as the source of happiness— as I gave power to the man who represented my destructive energy—was all-important. And it was magically becoming visible in the mirror and on the scales.

***

The life of restriction I was living, was becoming more and more evident in my appearance. Others were referring to me as being skinny, but I didn't feel to be. What I saw in the mirror didn't make me think I was doing anything wrong. I adored my bony hips that were starting to show and my behind that no longer existed. I felt good with my underwear hanging loosely around my frame. I thrived to no longer have the strong legs that once upon a time were classed as tree trunks but suddenly were looking like twigs— even if the muscles were defined. My weight had dropped and I had the same reaction as I'd had when I stood on the scales in March. I was shocked, but happy, relieved and loving myself. I hadn't been aiming to loose more weight. But now that I'd lost it, I wanted to maintain that mark of 42kgs, which was also the mark of love and happiness.

I needed something more though. I needed something extra that would make it easier for me to keep up the behaviour I'd been applying. Suddenly the rules and restrictions were becoming all-consuming and I felt to be loosing the mental ability I once had, when clinging to those rules and following them through. The lifestyle I was living needed to be tangible and my own obedient and disobedient behaviour needed to be monitored. The only thing I could think of to do was to put it in writing. This was an easy task, seeing as though since day one of being in Australia, I'd been writing about the people, the places, the work, the drinking and occasionally, the passing thoughts about food and exercise. Everyday of my travels had been recorded as I'd made it a routine to sit alone, once a week, desperate to avoid interruptions so as to spill my adventures onto paper. It was the first time in my life that I'd applied such discipline in regards to journaling. So choosing to take this form of expression to a different level—to Anna's level—was easy done and I felt it would guide me home safely, where my goal would be realized.

The rules I'd been living by, were now mine. They were what I owned, what I'd become and they would get me to where I felt I needed to be. They also needed venting, they needed air to breathe. I had to switch off any urges I had to unload my thoughts onto the people around me; this would've felt to be a selfish and shameful act and a burdening on the whole world. The urges I had, became the words that started flowing from my pen onto paper, instead of from my mouth into the heart of someone who may have listened, cared and who may have helped me. But I'd never have let anybody help me. I was an independent and strong individual and I had a reputation to hold in place. So the black notebook I chose, gave my life more sense and purpose. Life was bearable once I was able to express myself freely without judgement from anyone other than myself.

From then onwards I started living as if being in two worlds. My bright-coloured travel journal contained the tales of my daily life, my parties, my smiles, my energy and my happiness. My black-coloured notebook contained my inner life, which was my food intake, my alcohol consumption, my exercise. I expressed the positive actions I'd taken in order to realize my goal as well as the negative actions that were distracting me from my goal. I felt to be a part of one world but I was creating another.

For months I'd been working to establish this extra life inside of myself—the life of which my daily actions and my behaviour were an expression. And, as the kilos dropped, this inner world was becoming more and more apparent. Overriding thoughts were slowly becoming evident in my deeds, words and actions. 60,000 thoughts a day pass through the mind, but it's those most valued thoughts, the ones that are most significant, that turn into actions. To keep a journal, was to describe those thoughts. The thoughts I had, felt to be creating too many feelings and the actions I took, never felt to be reaching their potential, without taking a note of them. As soon as the black notebook became a part of my travels, I started seeing those thoughts written down and I knew everything I stood for in life was being stretched and pushed as far as was humanly possible. And I felt so safe and contained with the notebook. It became the leaking expression of anorexia.

Expressing anorexia in written word meant I didn't need to express it in any other form, especially not through speech. My spoken word never coincided with my writing. If anything, my spoken word concealed the world my pen was giving life to. Those who I was close to never suspected a thing. Even when speaking with my Mam and sisters on the phone, I managed to hide any problems by speaking openly about the weight I'd lost. So contradictive! But this is exactly how it was; I was open and claimed my new low weight was a result of healthy eating habits as well as hard physical work. They therefore believed everything was well in Niamh's world, just like I did. Talking so clearly about my low weight made everything seem okay. Convincing them that I was healthy was a way to convince myself of the same 'truth'. This conviction also made me feel safer when thinking of returning home. I felt they'd at least be prepared for what was to come because deep down I knew it would be a shock for them to see me so thin. This notion never stopped me from controlling my food intake and restricting, because I needed to hear from everybody that I was a winner. My whole year of backpacking had been in aid of returning home, full of life, travel stories and experiences, in a body that represented all this attained glory. And to make that happen, I had to keep living by the 'healthy' rules of Anna whilst keeping the lines of communication with the home front as open as possible, by claiming that my weight loss was due to different eating patterns. This way, I was being 'honest' yet secretive, all at once. It was perfect.

***

Saying I was returning home—which could've been Holland or Ireland—often made me feel like a failure. In my heart I wanted to travel, but I didn't want to be like the boozing backpackers anymore. At that point, I didn't know of how else I could travel if my experiences weren't revolving around parties and drinking. It was like I'd only ever been introduced to two ways of living: either travel and boozing OR living a 'normal' life in a structured manner. The dream of travel, which I felt to be neglecting by returning home, was a life I couldn't financially sustain anymore. I figured if I couldn't live one life, then all that was left was the other. I had to see the positive side of no longer travelling. By realizing the prospects of what a settled, controlled and regulated life could offer me, I was starting to feel safe. I could see how I'd be able to strengthen the guard that had been protecting me. I'd have routine, restriction and rules. I needed control and discipline. I too could prove my ability to be happy living a 'normal' life, just like everybody else. With this, I had a new goal! And so, I consciously chose to move to the country where I'd meet the friends who'd formed my past and who'd confirm me as being the winner. I chose Holland. It wasn't ONLY Anna's strength that was pushing me towards that country, in search of the controlled life that Dutch society represented in my mind. It was a different strength that was lagging behind Anna. That strength (in a very weakened state) wasn't in search of control or regulated living. It was in search of love, support and nourishment. Because, on the occasional fleeting moment when the haste of life temporarily eased, the tiniest little voice came from a very deep source and told me, 'Niamh, you have something you must sort out. There's something you need to attend to and it can only be done by surrounding yourself by your family.'

Two forces were guiding me away from travels and towards a life of discipline and a life where family stands for more than anything else. I knew there was some reason as to why I had to switch off to any other yearnings I still had inside of wanting to travel around this amazing planet and to be as free as a bird in flight. Still I was strong willed, so I insisted that my dreams were coming true by ending my travels. This personal persuasion was one of two things that let me accept the step I was taking back into the mundane life. The other factor that enabled my acceptance was the little black notebook. I knew that notebook had become the reason for my decisions. So I felt safe. I continued to smile to my friends and my family whilst the truth was being scribbled in ink.

Part II

 **1**

AUGUST 2008

20-08-07

*Right, well, it's the 20th of August and I've started to keep a food
diary. Everything I eat and the feelings that come along with that,
will be written down. It's strange how it has come to this. I don't
have a problem. I just read that a food diary is a positive thing to do.*

*My eating patterns are pretty bad. I try to starve myself. Well
not really. I don't have lunch, because I'm not hungry, even if I've
been running around at work. I don't even think that I could sit
down at lunchtime and eat a sandwich. It seems pretty gross to
me. How bad!!! The thoughts of putting two slices of white bread
in my body and then having a meal at dinnertime. It's disgusting.
And it disgusts me to see other people eating, especially now that
I'm working in a restaurant. I just think it's awful. How can those
people do it? Or even to sit down to a pizza and FINISH IT!!! Or
eat a whole plate of pasta? I wouldn't be able to. I used to, without
any problems, especially if I'd skipped lunch. I'd have a big dinner.
But even that has changed. Slowly but surely, I've been eating
less and less. People have started referring to me as being skinny.
Which I personally think is BS! I'm normal, I'm okay. I look in the
mirror and the person standing there is normal, some days even a
fat cow.*

*I eat my breakfast. It's low fat muesli with skimmed milk and
that's the meal I enjoy the most. At night I look forward to the
morning, because then I'm allowed to have breakfast. And it tastes*

so good. I always try to eat as slow as I can. Thirty minutes maybe. Because then I can tell that I'm not stuffing my face and therefore I'm not overeating. At work I don't eat. If I can do a nine-hour shift without eating, I'm fine. I'm still fast. I don't feel weak. I just have a coffee. Maybe two. The milk in the coffee fills me up. Big time! Especially if it's not skinny milk. Everyone always gives out to me about this. I order a skinny latte. But they think it's unnecessary. What the **** is their problem? It's got nothing to do with anybody what I eat and when I eat. Nosey &&$£"%^&!!!!

If I have a bad eating day, like when I pig out and can't stop myself, I need to make up for it the next day. So I'd have as much green tea as I can drink (sometimes it can be 3ltrs) and for dinner I'd have yoghurt with fresh fruit. I would purposely stay away from the kitchen. That way I avoid food. I would also avoid alcohol, because once I start drinking, especially beer, then I get drunk and all my good food behaviour goes out the window. And once I start drinking or eating, there is no stopping me. And it's so gross. I absolutely hate myself when I get like that. It happened last Thursday. I pigged out on crackers and dips, all because I'd been drinking too much alcohol. When you're so strict and don't eat a lot, you're body gets used to it. You can function properly. But if you give in, you can't control yourself, because your body needs this food and your brain is telling you to eat. That's when it gets out of control. I've never made myself sick after pigging out. So that's why I believe I have this under control. But the binging was probably the first sign that my eating habits aren't like most people's.

When I booze and then binge and then stop eating the next day and have at least two alcoholic drinks, I binge again uncontrollably and need to make up for it again the next day. So you see what kind of a vicious circle this is? And why? When did it start? Only since I came to Darwin. I think. When I was working in the pub I was eating two really healthy meals a day and I went to the gym and

did yoga. But what's happened since I left? It's the fact that I'm not
exercising. So I'm terrified of putting on weight. I'm not eating two
good meals a day anymore. Just one, if I'm lucky.

I never really binged before I came to Darwin. I never ate bad
foods. But here all I seem to do is eat crap. I really hate myself
for it. Why am I so scared of putting on weight? I don't know. It's
because everyone said, before I came to Oz, that I was going to
put on weight. I was looking so good when I left home. I weighed
around 48 or 49kgs. I didn't want to be one of those backpackers
that went to Oz for a year and came back massively overweight.
Disgusting! So I've been really strict. I've done so much physical
hard work which forced me to eat. But it was always healthy.
I banned bread, didn't eat meat. No heavy sauces. Just fruit,
yoghurt, cereal, soups, rice (plain) and noodles. I now weigh
42kgs. Well, the last time, it was 41. But I reckon I've put on at
least a kilo or two since then. Because I've been binging and doing
nothing, except for working. I've decided to focus on sports. I'm
going to do lots of different courses, I'm going to get extremely
active and make it my profession. I've got the willpower and the
motivation. I think I would be a good personal trainer! I think it
would be so cool to devote my life to sports, health and fitness.
I also reckon it's probably the only way I will be able to live and
eat normally. So if I work in a gym or work as a yoga teacher or
an aerobics instructor, I will allow myself to eat proper and, most
importantly, regular meals.

I dread the thoughts of being fat. Which I know will happen,
someday. It's probably the reason for me to go back home. I have
to avoid putting on weight. That sounds so bad. But I have to get
my body back on track. I need a normal lifestyle before this all gets
out of hand. It's the alcohol that's going to make me fat. And here
in Oz, I can't stay away from it. Being in constant holiday-mode,
it's nearly impossible not to drink everyday. So it's just wrecking
my body. I think if I'd stay in Oz longer, the alcohol would kill me.

*I haven't had my period for over six months. I'm also so scared
of everyone's reaction back home. It's going to be so controlling.
And whenever I think of what's waiting for me, I want to put on a
bit of weight. Just up to 45kgs (I probably am that at the moment).
Just to keep them from being suspicious or forcing me to put on
weight. Because that won't work! It's not going to work. It will
only push me in the other direction. ****! What am I going to do?
If I just keep eating healthy, then I won't want to binge and I won't
need to punish myself the next day, by not eating. It sounds so easy,
but it's hard to put it into practice. I also need to write down my
feelings when I'm trying to get back into normal eating habits.
So much goes around in my head. It's ruling my days. Not really
taking over. But it's playing a big part...*

24-08-07

*What the hell! Yesterday I worked nine-and-a-half hours. Before
work I had a bowl of muesli. At work I had a couple of coffees. I feel
bad for all this coffee. But I'm having it with soya milk. It's better.
I knew we were going to the markets, where there are hundreds
of food stalls. I knew I'd eat something small there. That's what
I planned. I had a vegetarian spring roll. But then things went
wrong, when a friend went and got me something. She got me a
chicken shaslick on a skewer. And it was absolutely disgusting and
fatty and greasy and tasteless. But I had to eat it because she bought
it for me. And I knew once I took the first bite, I would have wanted
to puke, to get that **** out of my body. . . NOW!!! I was being
polite by eating it. But I could feel the cholesterol and the fat being
absorbed into my veins. And there was nothing I could do to stop
it. It was too late. I'll be a fat cow. I was doing reasonably well.
But I'm always around people who constantly eat such disgusting
things! And if I don't eat it too, they nag me.*

28-08-07

I've been trying to stick to regular eating times. It's been going okay for the past three days, except for last night. I had a tiny piece of pizza which I hated myself for. An absolute pig is how I felt. But I figured I'd been running around work all day. I worked thirteen hours on a bowl of muesli, a muesli bar and a yoghurt with some fruit. So I had probably worked it off. Well I hope I did anyhow. This morning my stomach was hurting. When I woke up, it was like I could feel it shrinking together. Like a pulling and an itching feeling, where there would normally be hunger pains. I love that feeling! It makes me feel like I'm doing a good job and not putting **** into my body. How long do I reckon I could live on yoghurt and fruit and muesli?

I can't remember the last time I actually went food shopping. The only things I buy at Coles supermarket are milk, muesli, fruit, yoghurt and tea. Now and then I buy tuna, which I absolutely adore. I don't want to eat meat anymore. I want to eat fish and seafood and feel good about eating it and I want to feel healthy afterwards. I want to eat fresh veggies, salads, no sauces, no dressing (except for vinegar). If I eat out, it's got to be sushi. It's good, healthy and an alternative source of energy, if you don't eat meat. I want to go to the gym again. I want to be able to function properly without food. I want to have a gorgeous body, be energetic and fit. I can't bring myself to eat the bread I have in my food bag downstairs. I'm sitting here, on my hostel bed, worrying about how I'm going to feel about eating it. What am I going to do? I feel that I need energy. I need to be able to keep on running at work, as fast as possible. I have three more weeks of running and carrying heavy plates. I want to feel good about myself. I want to love myself.

01-09-07

I've been having pretty okay days. I've been able to stick to regular healthy meals and I haven't binged or eaten too much. I haven't stuffed my face without wanting to. Thank god. Monday night I did have a piece of pizza. Last night and the night before I wanted to, so badly, but I didn't give in. I had a muesli bar and it didn't make me feel like I had to make up for it today, by not eating until dinnertime. This is what I have to avoid. It's the feeling I'm NOT supposed to have. Because when I do have it, it's when everything goes wrong. That's when I end up feeling like I have to stuff my face again. And the circle keeps on going.

I also had two healthy proper dinners. Well, it was toast with tuna and lasagne, which I didn't feel guilty about eating. Good girl! Other than that, since Sunday up until today, I've been eating yoghurt and fruit for dinner. I sprinkled sustagen (which adds extra protein and energy) on it and it was really filling. So I reckon I am eating enough. Sometimes too much. It's awful though, because sometimes I'm in the kitchen or I'm in the supermarket and I can't believe the amount of food people eat! It's disgusting. The food on the shelves is far too much. Do people really need all this ****? And do they really eat it?

Working in a restaurant sometimes disgusts me. To see people stuff their faces like that! Oh no!!! Massive portions! And to think that it's just one of their three meals they'll be eating that day. Oh my god! Why is it such a problem for me? I don't know. It just is. But on the other hand, I love curry, spicy food, Thai food, pizza. I love it all. But I can't bring myself to eat it. Yesterday I had a small piece of tomato Italian bread. And I felt like I needed to drink a litre of water afterwards, just to compensate. Why, why, why?? How did it happen? I don't know. I just don't want to be one of those backpackers who comes home 50kgs heavier. I have lost weight, but I still don't feel as if I'm skinny, or slim. I'm normal. Just like everybody else. If people tell me I'm skinny, I take it as a

*joke. I don't listen and I don't believe them. I don't know. But I do
feel this journal is helping me. Because the last few days I haven't
been obsessing or stressing too much about what I'm eating.
It's too hot and muggy in the daytime to go running. I'm never
up early enough to go in the morning. But I'll get back into it, it
should be okay. I hope. And when I start doing a yoga or fitness
course I'll want to get fit and I'll need to eat properly. So it will all
turn out for the best. It will probably save me.*

05-09-07

*Feeling drained. I feel like ****. Too much alcohol! Not enough
proper food and nutrition. My energy levels are low. But I'm
scared. Of what? I have no idea. I need to weigh myself, badly.
%&££"$%!!!!!!!!!!!!!!!!! I keep on wanting to go to the
supermarket. Because that's what normal people do. But I'm there
and every little thing I put into my basket is too much. I analyze
everything. Today I bought fruit and yoghurt. And I thought,
'Why?' I picked up some tuna. I put it back on the shelf. I couldn't
buy it. I'd love to treat myself to bread. But I can't allow myself.
I can't buy anything but I'm obsessed with the supermarket, for
some reason. I automatically go and stand in front of the chocolate
and I'm drooling. The nuts, I'm drooling. And I hear voices inside
my head, coaxing me to walk away. And I do. Thank god! I analyze
what I have in my food bag, at the hostel. At the moment I have too
many nibbles. Rice-cakes and peanuts (so bad!). ****! Why did
I do that? Why did I buy them? Now I have to eat them. I bought
dates today. And I know I won't be able to control myself, once
I've opened them. ****! The bag is 500gms. They were cheap,
so I thought, 'Why not?' But I regret it already. Now I'm thinking
that I should have bought tuna and a bread roll. That would have
been yummy... Not to worry, tomorrow I'll have something to look
forward to.*

06-09-07

I didn't have the tuna roll. I just had sushi with chicken. I've had 3 bottles of green tea which is 4.5ltrs. I feel so weak. I don't know why. Usually I would eat less than I've eaten today and I would work harder. Today all I've done is eat. After breakfast I had a muesli bar, two pieces of chocolate, one sushi roll and now another bar. How disgusting. Maybe the green tea has cleaned out my system too much and there's nothing left inside of me? What a nice feeling that would be. O well, I'll keep on drinking the bottles. Who cares! I could have indulged in an ice-cream just then. But I didn't. I could have gone to the markets and stuffed my face, as usual. But I didn't. Good girl! I could have had another piece of sushi, but I didn't. So I'm not all bad!!!

14-09-07

I cannot believe how much I've just eaten. I had sushi a few days ago. I ate at the noodle house on Wednesday night. I couldn't stop myself. I pigged out so much. We had four courses and I ate until I was nearly exploding. I felt like a pig. Everyone had stopped and I was still going. Disgusting! I actually went to the bathroom afterwards, wanting to make myself sick. I wanted to vomit. There was somebody else there, she would've heard. So I didn't. I've never made myself sick before. Wednesday night I was so pleased that I didn't do it. I think once I start, I won't be able to stop. It will become a regular thing. It will seem so easy. Fighting it takes so much effort. If you can fight it and stop yourself, it can make you stronger.

***

In the darkness of the night, truths can be revealed. Sometimes it's more evident, sometimes it's more subtle, but awareness is needed in the waking hours, in order for dreams to serve their purpose in

terms of helping us with underlying issues. What my dreams were
starting to tell me, was that there was indeed a problem. I needed
to take action. Towards September 2007, I'd gone too far in the
race to achieve my goal. My behaviour was all-controlling. The
entries which I was devoting my free time to, were revealing the
awareness I had, but they were also revealing just how scared
I was. The behaviour I'd been applying from day one, was now
my way of life. It was no longer to be classed as being one single
achievement that would be recognized by sitting an exam, passing
with flying colours and receiving proof of succession in the form
of certification. Nobody was going to reward me with this goal
I'd accomplished. I didn't need a reward; the number on the
scales was rewarding enough. And in order to keep that rewarding
number close, the goal had slowly transformed itself from being
a destination to being a journey—a journey I'd convinced myself
that would show me the happy road so I could live a joyous and
free life. Little did I know where it was leading and so I gladly
witnessed how my goal had become my way of living.

By applying restricted behaviour, I subconsciously surrounded
myself with mental barriers, emotional blockages and physical
symptoms that were the manifestation of the illness that had been
waiting to enter my life. Throughout my backpacking year the
perfect triggers to trigger perfection were brought to me as they
were meant to. Anna was out to punish me, hence the reason for
control, during a time in my life that was meant to be magical.
Punishment is what I received for living my dream. Punishment
was becoming evident in my days, my decisions and my whole
life as it stood. However, that year in Australia, actually felt to be
magical! No matter how slowly she crept into my daily life, the
control didn't feel to ruin my adventure. I felt strong and mighty
in that control. I felt I was doing all the right things. So convincing
were these thoughts and so safe and secure were the feelings that

came along with the behaviour I was applying. To the world, I looked so proud, because pride is what I felt!

To say that my travels were the cause for the illness to take over or to blame other people's judgement, criticism and expectations, is far from the actual truth. Because the truth of the matter and thus, the truth of anorexia, IS extremely FAR! It's a deep truth. It was destined to come into my life. This was the perfect time. A destructive force of the psyche will only approach and attack when it hurts most, as it's a force that has the purpose to harm, to destroy and to ruin. Anorexia was a force that was waiting for the best time to hit me with all of its might. And throughout that particular year the development took over nicely. It was the perfect timing!

Leaving Australia in September, I felt I was doing the right thing even though I still longed for freedom. However, as a result of creating such a lifestyle within twelve short months, I'd slowly taken away my ability to live a free life. And on the 20th of September I was flying away from my dreams and towards my nightmares. My life was waiting and it was to take place in a prison cell that would be monitored, regulated and sustained by the guard within my psyche. I departed Australia and flew to Singapore first, where I was to spend a month travelling whilst feeling the pain of enjoyment and relaxation.

 **2**

SEPTEMBER 2007

21-09-07

I've had some really bad days this week. Again. I had a massive dinner on Monday night. Then I was afraid to eat for a day or two. When I went out for a goodbye dinner on Wednesday just before leaving Australia, I was able to control myself. Not like last week at the noodle restaurant. That was just over the top! Yeah, so this week, well, the past eight days, I've had two big dinners. The squid salad and the Thai rice. So gorgeous!

Now I'm in Asia for a month. So my patterns will change. Yesterday it was my first day. All I ate was dried fruit, nuts and freshly squeezed juices. I'd like to try a lot of different healthy foods. The amount of fresh fruit stalls, delicious! And dried everything, which is so healthy. Yesterday I bought a bag of dried tuna. I tried one bite and threw it away. O well, not to worry, it was different, overly salted and it nearly made me sick. I indulged in peanuts. But I enjoyed them so much. I'm still enjoying them right now. I'd like to try loads of stuff like that. I still have to have my first proper Asian meal. But I don't deserve it. Not just yet. In the next few days maybe. And all these bottled green teas! Not sure how much antioxidants are in them. But I'll try to find the best one. We'll see how it goes. I miss my yoghurt and fruit salads already. And the muesli is too expensive here.

22-09-07

*Oh no. I'm sitting here stuffing my face with a bagel. I'm in
Starbucks. For half the price I could have had something healthy
and I wouldn't feel guilty. **%"!!$£$%^&!!! I'm going to have to
walk it off now. No more food for the next twenty-four hours. I'm
such a *****! Why do I do this to myself? I'm a fat fat *****. All
those starches, calories and carbs. I've got lots of green tea. So
I can detox. Maybe I'll go to the herbal shop and get some more
detox stuff. I read about it yesterday in the museum.*

29-09-07

*Oh god, I've been having the worst food days ever. I've been trying
to be good. But there is just so much to eat all day long. It's in my
face all the time and it's everywhere. Different dishes, different
foods and it's driving me insane. Yesterday, I had a great day. Just
cornflakes and then drinks: juices, coffee and milk. I felt so in
control. Today I was doing well. I had a healthy vegetarian dish
for dinner with green tea. Then in the hostel I had fish. OH NO!!!!
It was fried. It just looked so good. I couldn't resist. It was a lot
and so greasy. Thank god I still had to walk to the station, which
was twenty minutes. That made me feel better. But I ate it around
two hours ago. And I'm still feeling ****. Now, tomorrow I'll just
be eating fruit. Well I'll try. The day after tomorrow is when I can
have a good Thai meal. Spicy rice, I guess. I will deserve it then.
Now, I don't. I'm a fat bitchy pig. All I seem to do is eat, eat, eat.
I should have weighed myself before I left Oz. Then I'd know how
much weight I'm putting on.*

01-10-07

*I'm trying my best to just eat healthy. Any food I eat is either fruit
or juices or steamed rice. Not fried. Yesterday I had my last plate*

of fried rice, for the next while. Now it's only steamed. Fried means grease, fat and it's disgusting, even though it tastes beautiful. The grease that's left behind on the plate just makes me want to puke. It's absolutely gross. O well, it was nice while it lasted. Just rice, seafood and salad from now on. I can do it. I want to be fit, but I'm so not at the moment! It's such a shame. O well, as long as I eat healthy, and not too much, I should be okay. Shouldn't I?! Won't I be okay? Oh god. No, it will be alright. Even though I think I'm piling on the pounds as I write this ****!!

10-10-07

I've been doing alright. A bit too alright, to my liking, meaning I'm convinced I've put on weight. I've been eating one proper meal a day. But I shouldn't because I'm not doing anything. All I've done for the last ten days is sit on my lazy backside. It's been great and I've had a ball. But once I get back to Phuket and Bangkok I'll be walking again. I'll walk for twelve hours, exploring the cities. And I'll deserve to eat. I still have to try some Thai curry before I leave and some particular fruits. And other dishes, maybe Thai soup. I can't seem to get enough of prawns. It's all I eat, with noodles or rice. And that's bad, because the rice is always fried. Oh no! I think I've realized what's been stopping me from putting on weight up until leaving Australia (because I've definitely put on weight since coming here). It's the green tea I drink, or used to drink, up until some weeks ago. I can't get my hands on boiling water here, which is so frustrating and I long for it! I love it so much. It cleans me out and I feel the difference after my first cup. I want it now!

15-10-07

I hate myself and the amount of food I've been eating for two days now. I just can't help myself. I've been hanging out with an English girl and an Irish guy. All they do is eat. So if I don't join them, it will look sussed. So I have to eat as well, even though I don't want to. And, it's my last few days with Thai food. Which I think might be a good thing. Because if I were to stay here much longer, I'd go back home, as big as a house. Anytime I eat I feel bad. I can't wait to start running again and doing yoga and just feeling active and eating on my own terms. I only want to eat when I want to eat. I don't want to eat because I have to hide something or cover something up. Understand? I don't like the way I'm feeling about food at the moment. I was doing so well up until I left Kho Phangnang. **** man! I bet I'm a whale. I'm a fat ugly ***** of a whale. What am I going to do? Why can't I keep away from the food? What's happening to me? I'm a possessed and obsessed person and I don't like it one bit!

17-10-07

My time in Asia is done. I'm on the plane and I was able to stop myself from making myself sick. I was so tempted, but I know so well that once I've done it I'll do it again and again and it will become a habit and that's when it will all get out of hand. I'm just sick of eating and I'm worried what's going to happen once I get back to Holland and start the normal life. I won't be able to determine what I'm going to eat myself. I don't want to eat pasta anymore or potatoes or bread. I want to eat rice, vegetables, salad, yoghurt, muesli, soup and fish. No meat, no mince, no fatty sauces.

Ma's going to go ballistic and it's worrying me, just the thoughts! How is everyone going to react? I know I've put on weight since I left Oz. I'm probably 43 now. So I weigh 6kgs less than last year. And she won't believe me when I tell her that all I've done is exercise and become aware of what I eat and why I eat. She won't believe me when I say that I've changed my alcohol intake by drinking low-carbohydrate beer and more vodka. It's a combination of all these things I reckon. I'm not unhealthy. I have *control. Well, at least if I can control what I eat and know what I'm eating, only THEN I'm fine and in control.*

Keeping track of my daily intake helps me so much. I don't know. But it's just getting to me. It's leading my life at the moment. Some weeks are better than others. If I can resist ****** and fatty foods, then I'm okay. And when I'm doing other stuff, I'm grand. It takes my mind off of it. Like when I was working at the Italian restaurant. I did keep track of my food intake then but I was good at it. So I hardly ever felt guilty about what I was eating. I was having regular meals, they were healthy and I was always preoccupied with other stuff. On the island of Kho Phangnang, for a week, I was really good. I was eating healthy, and not too much. So I wasn't feeling guilty or shitty about putting something in my mouth. I don't know whether to tell anyone about any of this. How will they react? I'm scared. I don't want to have to listen to everyone giving out to me about it. It's too confronting. And worrying about it probably answers the question: Do I or don't I have a problem?!!! Anybody with any amount of brains can figure that out when reading this.

***

Travelling Asia stood as a period of transition. I was smack bang in the middle of closing of one chapter and opening another. But I was taking everything I'd created with me—all that I'd created in my inner world. Throughout my transition, I was facing something that scared me beyond belief. In Australia I ignored the fears whenever they arose and I punished myself for having insightful moments that were telling me to fix my life. I didn't see as much in Australia as I did when I was on the Thai beaches. In Australia I was distracted from my hunger, my cravings, my pain and my physical state by the busy life I forced myself to live. In Asia I had little to steer my thoughts away from my truth. I did all

I could but my visions were showing me that home was coming closer and closer. This caused such panic and I was becoming aware that I had to put right the wrong I'd done. Which 'wrong' was that though? Was it the 'wrong' that loved ones would have seen—which was the weight I'd lost? Or was it the 'wrong' that Anna was seeing—which was eating food and letting myself enjoy a free life?

How was I meant to put both things 'right' at that point in time? To undo what my family would have witnessed as being damage, I wanted to eat normally, to feel fine with food and I wanted to gain a few kilos. To undo what Anna witnessed as being damage, I wanted to eat less, keep the weight off and have control over everything—mainly my food intake.

How was I able to satisfy the two worlds? How was I able to now cope with what I'd created? I was confused, scared and at a loss. I was torn between the voices of the world and the voice inside my head, which constantly made me wonder, 'To eat or not to eat?'

Up until that point I'd been far away from home. I was distant and I was strong. I'd been on my own and was only surrounded by amazingly loving friends who didn't know me as I was before. Friends had never seen my REAL appearance of health and nobody knew I'd lost 8kgs in the space of thirteen months—without needing to loose any of them. Whilst being away from home I'd attained the freedom to create my own inner world and my own magic, and that's exactly what I did. Suddenly it didn't feel to be magic anymore. This is why my panic was rising. I needed to turn back time and I had to gain weight, but I was terrified. I didn't know what was right and wrong anymore. My desire felt to be the right thing to pursue, which was to do everything in my power to be the happiest and healthiest I'd ever been. I had to continue to project to my surrounding world that I was naturally slim and that

I ate properly. In such confusion it was safer to keep on following the direction that had been feeding me my energy, strength and feelings of worthiness. I knew what I had to do. I had to keep others out of my inner world—which I'd already subconsciously been doing with the friends I'd been associating with. But, the new start in Holland meant there was a different level of distancing required.

***

Nearly thirteen months after leaving, I returned home. By boarding that plane to Holland and by letting myself be controlled by my own destructive inner voice, which was needing to prove to the world I was 'normal' yet 'different'—'normal' for being able to settle down and live a life surrounded by stability and 'different' for not returning as the backpacker who had gained weight—my fire was being put out. Was the fire in my soul actually still burning when I was returning home? Was there still a burning passion inside and was I still thriving on life? The fire keeping my passion for travel alive had gone out some time ago. At that point, I was doing my best to keep myself appearing to be thriving on the highs of life. Really I wasn't. Of course, I still felt that proof of my thriving feelings was visible in what I was undertaking and in how I appeared. My passion for life was visible in the energy I had and the smile that everyone saw continuously plastered on my no longer glowing face. I was so strong with my new behaviour that I'd convinced myself of owning an unlimited supply of energy and I didn't need the 'normal' amounts of food to sustain this level of energy. I simply needed 'different' amounts of food. Because 'different' is what I wanted to be.

More and more anorexia was becoming me. I was lost. My physical body was starting to feel the pain. My energy was low and feelings I thought I had, weren't feelings at all. They were thoughts fuelled by Anna. To feel any feelings and to deal with any issues, a person needs to stop and become aware. My awareness was evident in the little black notebook. But that's where it stopped. I wasn't able to bring it any further. I was in a race, so I had no time to waste and no urgency to engage in such a thing as confusing and confronting emotions. There was too much going on in the world around me and I needed the outer world to give me the much needed boosts of energy to keep me preoccupied from what was really going on within me.

The voice of destruction was now a part of me and it was the reason for every decision I made in life. That voice was my reason for returning. That voice had convinced me Holland was where I would be happy. That voice wanted me to seek happiness in proving to the world that I owned the strength of the world, and so much more. That strength was the power behind this voice. It came from somewhere deep. It was Anna's voice. It was Anna's power. With that voice in my ear, I felt I was invincible.

Even though I was invincible, I was scared of what people would think of me. This fear only urged me to eat less and to restrict more. I didn't want to loose and abandon the new way of living that had made me so happy throughout my travels. It didn't matter that I'd reached a point where my new way of living was making me panic. I figured if it had once made me happy, then it would surely make me happy again! As long as I continued to follow the rules and tighten them as I went through my days. And if I was showing a happy face, wouldn't everyone believe that I'm happy and wouldn't they also feel happy? I figured this was the logical conclusion. My new look was living proof that travelling made me happy.

The rising fears were a sign that something was wrong. Questions of doubt were racing through my mind, 'Would they be happy to see that I'm different? Would they be pleased to see that

I'm a new and improved Niamh? How would they react? Would they love me more? Would they support me, just like they did during our telephone conversations?' My questions were answered as soon as I walked through the gates at arrivals.

***

I was welcomed back to Holland in manner I'll never forget. Nor will anybody else. The whole family had come to Amsterdam to pick me up. Four of my most precious friends came to welcome me as well, with a big banner in tow! I was blown away, overwhelmed and tears were all I could produce. Tears weren't only coming from me but also from my sisters and Mam. However theirs weren't of joy but instead for the shock of what I'd become within thirteen months. I didn't realize it at the time. Or maybe there was a tiny feeling of recognition. Did they comment on my weight? Of course they did. But the remarks were only subtle during the first few days of being back in Holland. I brushed off their concern and I had my health stories at the ready, with the aim of convincing them of my 'truth'. They could see my excitement, my smile and my eagerness to start over. I was full of travel stories and I was eager to share, eager to re-connect and eager to get my life into gear!

After a few days, my Mam asked if there was anything else going on with my weight. She forced me to stand on the scales and the magic number was 41! I was delighted, but didn't show it too much. Mam was worried but I managed to ease her worries with my health stories once again. Everything was going to plan! She urged me to see the doctor so as to get some tests done. Her words of concern were the words I needed to hear in order to strengthen the force that was at work within. My Mam said so strictly, 'Niamh, you're going to be putting back on all that weight you've lost!' I can still hear, to this day, the voice inside my head shouting,

'I MOST CERTAINLY AM NOT!' However the only words that came from my mouth were, 'Yes, okay.' Such expectations and pressure was doing more harm than good. It was perfect however because it meant the decisions I was about to make, would be based on the desire to support Anna's needs. The voice inside my head was far louder than the subtle yet truthful whispers that came from a different source telling me I was in need of help. Subtle whispers were too easily ignored, especially when the world around me was shouting the perfect words my inner controlling voice was longing to hear. Inside and outside of my head the voices were shouting in unison—a duet was being performed—and the song was singing out loud and clear that distance, isolation and loneliness were the only way in which I was able to survive this life. There was no turning back.

 **3**

OCTOBER 2007

23-10-07

Oh no, it's all getting a bit too much. I can't take it anymore. This is a problem and I have to solve it myself. But I don't think I can. There's nobody I can turn to. I don't know how to do this. It's almost compulsory I put on as much weight as possible, as quickly as possible. Everybody is watching me. They are all looking. I just want a normal life, with a routine so I can eat regularly. I want to decide what I'm eating. Nobody understands what I'm going through. This is so hard. But actually it's a brilliant move; coming back to Holland. If I would have stayed away longer, I would have become worse. This is such a hard period. I don't know if I can solve this. My stomach hurts so much when I eat.

Nobody is treating me normally. I'm a freak. That's how I feel. Ma is treating me strangely too. As if I'm ill. Everybody is tiptoeing around me. They're all being careful. Yeah, it frustrates me so much…

I'm taking as many vitamins as possible, just so my bloods are healthy, for when I go to get them checked. I'm being forced to go to the doctor but I'm not going to say what's exactly going on. The more I say it to myself, the more I'm going to start believing it. So I'll solve this alone. I can do this without a doubt, once I have my life back on track. I'll just eat lots of vegetables, fruit, rice and noodles. As long as I'm eating healthy, then I can stay on top of this. And if I do put on some weight, I can get active again and I'll have more energy. It will be brilliant!

It's not fair that I'm being forced to eat this ****, just to fatten up! I'd love to tell someone. But no, I can't. And I'm not going to tell Ma. I would have shown her this little black notebook because I wanted to talk to someone about it. But now I can't and I don't know why. It's me against the world, as per usual. The more people who force me to eat, the more I'm going to resist. They're pushing me away. I really want to be in Breda now, where I can get a job and have my own place. So I can just be myself. I don't know what damage I've done to my body. I don't want to know. I'm so full of food and I'm stuffing myself. I'm ugly. I see everybody looking at me. It's embarrassing. I've never felt so thin, so disgusting or so ugly before in my whole life. Why is that? It's so annoying. Is this how it's going to be forever? Every time I eat, every time I go to the toilet I'm being stared at, observed and seen as a freak. I hate it so much. I hate it. I hate it. I hate it. What have I done to myself? I've damaged myself and it's up to me to fix myself.

27-10-07

What's been happening the past few days? I've been trying to keep away from overeating. It's so strange. My feelings are so contradictive. I know I must put on weight. I actually WANT to put on weight.

Last Sunday I weighed myself: 40.5kgs. But now, I think I've put on 4kgs since then. I don't want it to happen so fast. I want to put on just a few kilos. But that can't happen from one day to the next! It can't be good for my body if I suddenly stuff my face.

You hear about people having an eating disorder. They go from one extreme to the other. I don't want to be like that! 45kgs. That's all. That's what my weight was when I was working in the pub in Australia. I don't want to weigh anymore than that! But on the other hand, I'm seeing people who I haven't seen in years. I don't want them to judge me. And that's probably what's going to

happen. I'm not looking forward to that. Maybe this is one of the
reasons why I'm not yet meeting up with everybody.

I don't mind going to the doctor, because I feel fine. Maybe my
iron is low. But I've been taking all of my vitamins, for two weeks.
So within three weeks I'll be even healthier. It's so strange. I've
been so good at dinnertimes. They aren't big portions. I'm just
happy that I'm eating, full stop! During the first days back in
Holland, I wasn't eating a lot during the day and I was fine to sit
down at the dinner table and eat in the evening. This is so good.
At the moment, all I do in the morning is drink. I don't eat. This is
so good. I only need to eat when I'm hungry, right? And if I want
to do yoga in the morning, I need to keep my stomach as empty as
possible. Isn't that a blessing! My breakfast is around noon, then
nothing until dinnertime. After dinner I don't eat anything else.
Last night I had something bad: half a scone. Other than that,
I haven't eaten anything in between. Well done Niamh! How can
I be hungry if I'm doing nothing all day? Even if it is cold outside
and I'm supposed to eat more to keep myself warm... Sitting
around all day long and just eating, wouldn't that make everybody
feel fat, yuck, lazy and unhealthy, no matter what size they may be?
Anyhow, if I keep this up, I'll slowly get back to my healthy self.
I'll keep taking my vitamins and I'll slowly but surely put on some
healthy weight. Time will tell.

21-11-07

Wow, it's been ages since I've written. That's a good sign. Yesterday
I went to the doctor. And I have to have my blood tested soon. The
eating is going okay, even though I still don't want to eat three
meals a day. I just can't do it. I might want to, sometimes, but
I can't. I don't feel I need three meals. In a week and half I'll be
starting my new job at the travel agency. Then I'll finally have a
routine. I'll be living on my own, so I can choose what and when

*to eat. I know I want to eat healthy. I have to eat. My body needs it.
That's something I've learned and I can't just go for a day without
eating. Not the way I've done so many times before. The damage
you do to your body is unreal, even the long term damage. You
wreck your body. I've only been practising extreme behaviour for
a few months. I was just in the nick of time. I even knew this when
I was travelling. I knew I had to come back home, to regain my
health. I knew it was the only way for me to solve this problem. I'm
working on it. I weigh myself every week at the same time. I'm still
the same weight as I was when I came back from travelling. 40kgs.
I don't know if this was my weight when I left Oz and went to Asia.
Maybe it was a few kilos less. What a bummer! I can soon cook for
myself and keep this under control, then everything will be fine!
Then I'm fearless. Nevertheless, I know it's going to be a problem
forever. Oh well, that's tough luck for me!*

26-11-07

*Last night there was something on the television about anorexia.
Apparently it's not an illness but a lifestyle! But it can get out of
control. Well, some things I could identify myself with. Like the
weighing scales. Constantly. My sister Orla has one now and
I want to be standing on it, all the time! Yesterday I stood on it
twice. The difference between the two times, was 0.2kgs. The
second time the weight was more than the first. I shouldn't do that
really. I should only weigh myself once a week, at the same time,
in the morning before breakfast, either on a Saturday or Sunday.
Then my weight would be the highest, because usually I'd be
drinking beer.*

*I'm starting to think along these lines: if I can see cooking as a
hobby, then I'll happily prepare it, and enjoy eating it. I'm looking
forward to it. Am I now falling back into my old pattern? I'm so
convinced that if you don't do anything, then you don't need food.*

But I know full well that this is BS. But it's just in my head and I can't just get it out, just like that! I can't. I don't know anymore. All I know is that I don't want to put on weight. I'm terrified of becoming obese. That's not how it's supposed to be!!!! We'll see how the following weeks go.

***

Six weeks after arriving back in Holland and my life was set. I knew in order to maintain the creation of my inner world, which was becoming apparent to those around me, it was vital that a distance was kept. Isolation was needed for the process of creation not to get disrupted.

My dream was becoming a reality. Every single thing I'd set out to do was now my way of living. I moved away from the family and had my own bedsit and a stable job in a travel agency where I could punish myself day in day out with the thoughts of being the gateway travellers needed in order to depart the country, all the while sitting in silent misery behind the computer screen. I had the stable, secure and most perfect life! I had the normality I'd been aiming for. I was just like everybody else and I only needed six short weeks to reach that goal! That was way too easy. Was I happy? No, I was miserable. Would I admit it? I did no such thing! Would I continue to live life? I was eager.

Holland was providing the necessities for the manifestation of the eating disorder to take over my life, with such intensity. It was perfect. I had placed myself back within a society that thrived on rules, structure, routine, regulations. What more could I have wanted? Nothing, surely! I was living the life of misery I deserved and now I had to suffer. It was brilliant! I also had the family convinced of my health and seeing as though they knew me better than anybody else, having them on board, meant I also had the world on board!

My entries were speeding up the process of letting the illness reach its peak as fast and as furious as was physically possible. It was only when I reached Holland and had everything I wanted to achieve, that I was using the words 'eating disorder' and 'anorexia'. These words were suddenly being spoken of when I felt I had nothing else to live for. They had initially only been floating around in my head, throughout the last months of my travels. But by this stage, they needed more ventilation. In the dark dreams I had at night there were visions that caused me to spill my 'truth' throughout the gloomy hours of the day, from my subconscious mind onto the pages of my black notebook.

Reaching the stage where I admitted to myself that I had the potential of an eating disorder wasn't enough for me to take action and seek help. The outside world was convinced there was nothing wrong, due to my words. This meant the inside world didn't feel the need to go against what others believed to be true. So the drive became more powerful and needed more and more fuel in terms of approval, succession, achievement, accomplishment, satisfaction and the creation of whatever it was that Anna wanted.

***

Anna wanted me to be nowhere, yet everywhere, all at once. Of course I still yearned to travel and I needed more satisfaction and achievement. As the kilos dropped, I felt this wasn't enough. Another goal is what I set for myself to accomplish, once I'd settled into my Dutch lifestyle. Yes, this new goal was Mexico! I wanted to travel to Mexico! This, I figured, would push me in many different ways. It was what I needed. It would give me freedom again. I truly believed I would be happy, once I reached that goal of Mexican travels, by November 2008. For the sake of satisfaction, more restrictions and punishment were mine. They appeared to be very similar to those I'd welcomed into my life back in Darwin when

I was working towards my trip to Asia; I desperately started saving every cent and this then strengthened my desire not to purchase food and not to eat properly. And to earn cash, I needed to stay working as I did, regardless of the fact that it made me unhappy. Feeling down I figured was simply a part of life!

The illness was well and truly leading my life. Skinny is what the world labelled me as being. But anorexic? Not quite yet. People saw me eating and therefore were reassured that there was no illness. It's the stereotypical judgement of the world. People hear 'anorexic' and instantly assume the patient doesn't eat anything at all. But I was eating even though I had the illness. I gave such importance to the stereotypical view. I believed that if everyone regarded anorexia as only being suffered when the person in question wasn't eating, then I was fine. The voice inside my head was happy to listen to the world! I told myself, more times than not, that there wasn't a problem. Telling myself I was fine confirmed my new way of living was my destiny. I was invincible and I was everything and so much more. Yet I was nothing—all at once. Like a magic trick: the truth is only revealed after the act is performed.

4

DECEMBER 2007

05-12-07

It's weird, but the past few days haven't been going well. Why? Because I had chips on Friday night. But if I didn't eat them, someone might suspect something, which is so stupid really because I'm the one who decided to put them in my mouth. It felt disgusting. I could feel that I was abusing my body. I felt it in my stomach, the grease felt so heavy, it was gross. I felt it in my intestines. I felt so bad. I drank as much water as possible afterwards, just to feel better. But I didn't feel better. I felt fat, I felt tired and I was in a bad humour because I could have said no. But I didn't and that's why I hated myself. I have been pigging out. I swear to god I am never going to eat chips ever again, or anything greasy. Never, ever again. And the worst thing about the whole chip-scenario was that I couldn't stop once I'd started eating them.

The next day I had a sore stomach. And I was still angry that I'd eaten them. It took me twenty-four hours to shake off the bad feelings. I then felt I needed to starve just as punishment for abusing my body with such grease. But my mates only seem to want to eat. Why is it that a person's day revolves around eating? Why? Why can I not shake the feeling of disgust? I get this awful feeling when I see people walking around town, stuffing their faces. Why does it make me think of people in a bad way? Why is it that whenever I think about eating with someone, I don't want to and

I feel pressurized? Why do I not enjoy my food when I'm eating with others? Why is it that I have the tendency to stuff my face when I know I've had way too much food? Being full doesn't stop me from eating. Why is it that I can't stand the fact that the people eat ****? And why is it that when my friends put loads of spread on their sandwich, all I can think about are the fats, greases, calories, sugars and toxins they're putting into their system? Why is it that whenever I don't do anything, I feel I shouldn't need to eat?

All these questions can be answered with one simple answer: I'm obsessed with food. I'm not going to say I've got an eating disorder, because I do eat.

This week I might detox. But I'm not too sure what I'm allowed to eat or drink. I think it's only juices. How nice! Just to flush out all the ****. I have to be good until Friday because we're going out for dinner and I swear I'm not eating chips! OH NO! I'm not doing it!! ****, we've said we're going to make cocktails. Calories!! NO!!! And then... beer? I don't want it. What am I going to be like on Christmas day? Bad, real bad! Will I be able to enjoy it? If I eat in small portions, I shouldn't feel too bad. So far I've been good. Anytime I've felt fat, I have thoughts of making myself sick.

As I write this, I know what I'm saying and I know I have the potential of creating an eating disorder. But I've never made myself sick. No matter how tempted I've been. I'm able to say no to the urges I have because it's bad for my teeth and throat. I also know that if I do it once then I'm definitely going to do it again. That's what an English backpacker told me. She used to do it. She said that once you start it, you realize how easy it is and then you do it all the time. I'm not going down that road. If I do, it will be harder to get back to normal. I'm good as long as I have this under control and if I choose what I put in my mouth. I'd love to just eat yoghurt at lunchtime too, with muesli. But I can't. People would start making comments and I don't want that. It's the hardest part of wanting to eat like this—hearing comments from others and feeling their suspicions. Not that I have anything to hide!

Last Friday, nine days ago, I had some cake. Bummer! I didn't want it, but otherwise I would have gotten strange looks off others. Then I thought, 'Oh no, now I have to eat my two slices of bread!' I only ate one. Maybe if I take a juice instead of a slice of bread, for lunch? Will that work? I'm going to try that tomorrow. I'll take two slices of bread and a cup-a-soup. If one is enough, I'll throw the other in the bin. Can I do that? I think so. But what if the soup and one slice of bread isn't enough, and I eat two? Then I'll have eaten far too many calories. That's not my intention! So what's the wise thing to do? I can do anything...

I look disgusting at the moment. I wonder if there's anything wrong... Can there be anything wrong? It will be okay. I'll let you know about the detox!

24-12-07

Well, it's Christmas Eve. I've done so well the past week, knowing that Christmas is just around the corner and that I'm going to put on massive amounts of weight. I was 39kgs the other day (Saturday the 22nd). I don't know if that's because I was going to the toilet so much that day. I went four times and that would always affect my weight straight away. Just like eating food affects my weight straight away. I can be a kilo heavier or lighter. This can be very deceiving at times. But after eating only small amounts of muesli each morning, two slices of bread for lunch and four proper dinners per week, I've done pretty well not to have put on weight. Especially now that I'm doing nothing but sitting behind the computer at work, all day long. Maybe the yoga helps. It makes me feel so good and flexible. Yesterday I did it really well, forty minutes, after my breakfast, which means I didn't feel any dizziness! And I had more energy and was able to focus better.

*Even though they say that yoga should be done before breakfast.
O well, as long as the food has been digested then it shouldn't
interfere with anything.*

*What's going to happen tomorrow? Is everyone going to be
checking if I'm eating? Am I going to have to stuff my face just to
prove that I don't have a problem? But surely that's ridiculous!
That leads to bulimic behaviour. You stuff your face so much, just
to disguise the fact that you don't want to be eating ****** and
fatty food. That's not good! I'm the boss of what I put in my mouth.
I'm the only one who decides what and when and how much food
I eat. Nobody else. It's me that's going to feel bad afterwards. I'm
the one who has to feel that feeling and deal with it. Nobody else.
Right, can I just enjoy Christmas day without all this ****? I hope
so. Time will tell. I'm going to go on a detox afterwards anyhow. O
well, we'll see what happens.*

30-12-07

*I survived. I did so well and I'm proud of myself. I don't care how
stupid everyone thinks this is. Even though it was Christmas day,
I'm so happy that I didn't ruin my day by overeating. I didn't spoil
my dinner by overeating chocolate. I didn't get any **** in my
stocking, thank god! I enjoyed my dinner immensely. I even ate
some of the fry. So nobody noticed a thing. I had some ice-cream
too! Not a lot, but I enjoyed it. Everyone else stuffed their faces,
or so it seemed. Chocolate galore. But I wasn't tempted. I had
four pieces throughout the whole day. I enjoyed the ones I ate and
didn't feel guilty and I knew I didn't want more. If it would have
been nuts, it would have been a different story. That's when I start
and can't stop. It's not the same with chocolate or ice-cream or
crisps. I can have a taste and then stop. I'm able to resist them real
easy, without any effort! This gives me a feeling of being in control.
It's great!*

Since Christmas day I've had three biscuits and one proper dinner last night, for which I'm now suffering. I'll have to make the twenty hours without food now. I'm just not hungry either. I ate at 8pm last night. It's now just after midday so I've only three more hours to go. And that's so easy. I've been up since 8am. I've been purposely keeping busy so I will be burning the calories I ate last night. I did fifty minutes of yoga. But if I go to a friend's house for dinner, I'll have to go longer without food. Maybe I'll make the twenty-four hours. As long as I keep myself busy, my mind doesn't stray towards food.

It makes me sick to my stomach when I see my colleagues drinking cans of coke and eating bars of chocolate day in day out. That's all they do and I can bet you anything that they don't walk forty minutes a day nor do they do twenty minutes of yoga nor do they eat healthy dinners. Pigs! How can they feel good about themselves? All they do is stuff **** into their bodies. The amount of toxins! A friend said to me last night that once my body gets used to my new eating patterns, I'm going to put on weight. Well, not if I have anything to do with it!! I'm not like them. People don't know what I eat. Absolutely nobody knows the amount of calories I put in my mouth everyday. Even I don't. I just know it's as little as possible. Haha!!!! This means a detox for me again—fruit and vegetables without sauces. Vitamins are all I need. Bring it on!

14-01-08

I'm sick to death of people asking me what I eat during the day or what I ate for dinner. It really does my head in. Big time! Once the fat has passed my lips and entered my system, I know I have to get it out. How do I do that? I just compensate with buckets of water and green tea and I eat as little as possible the next day. This cleans out my body. It's really good as well to drink lots of soup. It contains only 5 calories and it cleans out your system too. Some *people treat their body like dustbins. Constantly they put **** in it. How can they live with themselves? I don't want to eat just to please other people and then feel guilty for three or four days, like I'm now still feeling bad for eating that pizza on Saturday night. ****!*

I'm just sick and tired of it. Of what though? What is IT? I can't bring myself to write it. It's ruling my life, there's no denying it. But my face has gotten big and fat. Why? Another thing I don't understand. It's gross and I look like ****. Because I'm just so disgusting. My hair, my wrinkles, the whole lot. I've had it. Absolutely. I don't want to eat anymore.

06-02-08

Well, it's been a while. Is that good or bad? It depends on what way you look at it. For my body or my weight? They have become two separate issues. Usually what's good for my body (healthy food and not stuffing my face) is good for my weight (doesn't everyone want to loose weight?!). But for me, I don't know anymore. The last time I weighed myself I was around 38.8kgs. I wasn't shocked, or maybe a little. I actually thought I'd gained a few kilos. I must be eating healthy. Every time anybody offers me a chocolate, I can't resist. I don't know why. To disguise it maybe. So nobody thinks that I don't want to eat ****. Even though I don't want to eat it. But I do, but I don't. I feel so bad and then I don't want to eat anything for the rest of the day. Then I get so hungry that I overeat the next time I eat.

But I don't throw up. I've stopped myself many a time. I'm disciplined because I know I will have passed the point of no return. I've stuffed my face and drank far too much beer the past few weeks. When I look at my friends, it makes me feel sick the speed at which they eat. I feel bad for thinking like this. But I can't help it. Food should be natural. Putting **** in your body is bad *and it makes you feel bad. Your digestive system gets out of whack. My friend had five chocolates on Sunday night. I only had one. I couldn't believe it. And then she had a sausage roll before we went home. Disgusting! My god! How bad am I? Oh well, the next while I'm only to have food with goodness and I'll try not to feel awful whenever I see people stuffing their faces.*

20-02-08

Sometimes I hate myself, other times I don't. Sometimes I wish I'd put on weight and other times I feel gross when I eat the smallest little thing. I feel the discomfort whenever I eat something that's unhealthy. I feel what it does to me and the bad effects it has on me. Am I going to get back to normal? Are my healthy eating patterns affecting the way I function; my brain, my thinking, my attitude, my approach to life in general? What am I going to do? Is there anyone I can talk to? Sometimes I see the way people look at me. I don't want them to think I'm a freak. Does everyone know and they're just afraid to say something to me about it? I'm 38kgs. I weighed myself at Emma's. I was there for a day and a night. I stood on the scales three times. Why? I'm frightened of putting on weight. What am I going to do if I do? I cannot bring myself to eat more than I already eat. I really don't want to eat at all. Can I beat this feeling all by myself? What's going to happen if I'm confronted? Will I be able to admit? Will I come out and face facts? How come, when I was in Darwin, I was able to live on a bowl of muesli and a muesli bar and fruit and yoghurt? How did I do that? You'd think that it would be harder to do physical work on that small amount of food, than doing brain work on nothing? It should be easy to do brainwork on nothing. All I'm doing is sitting on my behind, walking forty-five minutes and doing twenty minutes of yoga. It's nothing. Why do I need to always be active? What am I going to do? How and when will this all stop?

***

As time progressed, two worlds were gradually becoming one. In these early stages of the illness the contradicting energies within my psyche, the one that was out to destroy and the one that was out to heal, were being heard. To witness these two energies, as an outsider, shows that the battle had already commenced and the strongest would win. At that time it was simply too soon for me to admit to anything that could've been classed as defeat and failure. In my strength I kept on living the life I needed. I was giving all of my power to Anna and ignoring the moments of clarity that told me I needed help. With my ignorance, the world around me was slowly becoming less significant. I was living a busy life and it was how I felt I needed to be—in my desperation to travel. I disguised the illness and still used the same convictions I'd been using when I returned from Australia. In order to keep both worlds apart, I had to isolate myself more and more from the surrounding world. Yet I was able to force myself to thrive. I was still smiling to the world and I was still able to project myself as being the bubble of energy, even in my weakened body. The projection and conviction of my health was of utmost importance if I wanted to keep on satisfying the longing I had to eat as little as possible. This projection and conviction kept me safe, sane and strong in my actions to continue feeding what had now become the addiction. The gene I'd been given, which I never knew was within me, subconsciously needed more satisfaction. Satisfaction was only gained, by the weight that either stayed the same or, preferably, became less. Satisfaction had once been a guarantee when achieving such brilliance and this was what I still aimed for. There was no way I could have let this go, not until I had that amazing feeling once again. I was aiming for the high that would send me flying into my own world, letting me soar so far away from this planet so I'd never want to fully engage in anything anymore!

My inner world was about to become more obvious to the outside world. The fire burning inside my soul—resembling my dreams and my passions—should have been setting off sparks of brilliance. However, there was nothing BRILLIANT taking place in my life. I was starting to doubt my strength and my ability to travel in the outside world. The goal of going to Mexico was something that had been set and needed to become a reality, with the fuel of Anna. As I weakened, that exact same fuel was making my travel dream more challenging than I imagined. In my struggle, I felt it wasn't enough to resist food and to save money, so I decided that I had one more task to accomplish, before making it to Mexico by November 2008. I took on the tour-guiding job again, with the same company I'd worked for two years previous in Ireland and I would happily work during the holidays I was given from the travel agency in Holland. I planned to fly to Ireland on the 1st of June and stay for three weeks to guide three tours. This would provide me with the funds I desperately needed so as to fly to Mexico and leave my little imprisoned life behind. In preparation for these tours, I needed to undergo months of study, in my spare time. My friends were urging me not to take on so much. They figured I needed to chill-out! But I felt that was for losers. Who needs to relax in their spare time or when they have their holidays? That's pure torture, right!? I was independent and followed through what I'd set out to do. I knew what I wanted, I knew what I could achieve and so, it would forever be me against the world.

MARCH 2008

04-03-08

I spoke with my cousin Sandra on Friday night. I didn't say so much. But she made me see sense. Somehow. She gave me tips on how to put on weight. I know that I've gone too far and the longer it goes on, the worse it will get. The more weight I loose, the more I'll WANT to loose. I'm pretty sure that I've put on weight the past few weeks, but I've realized I need to eat more. I've realized that it's affecting me because I have no energy, no sense of adventure, no drive and no enthusiasm. Usually I always have these things. But now all I'm concerned about is becoming obese. What will happen then? I'll go from one extreme to the other. I've heard that it can happen and it terrifies me. I know I can become healthy again, full of life and energy—in a healthy way. I'll eat more fruit and more vegetables. I'll eat small portions throughout the day. I'll make my stomach bigger, ever so slowly. Right now, I look in the mirror and I absolutely hate myself. I've got a massive fat face, with chubby cheeks, a fat gross ugly head with wrinkles and a massive amount of hair. My clothes are ****, I'm afraid to spend money on anything new because then it might be too small. So I'm looking unhealthy, drained and awful. I know it's going to be so hard for me to get back to normal and to NOT let my life revolve around what I eat. Everyone reckons I've lost more weight since returning from Australia. I don't know. I feel as if I've been eating more.

Yesterday I felt strong about it. I felt that I'd be able to get better and I'd get back to normal. Surely I'll be able to conquer this thing just for the fact that I've admitted to myself that I need to regain the lost weight? I'm going to stay active and I'm going to keep up my yoga. I'm going to start rollerblading. I'd love to run a marathon but I don't have the physical strength to train at the moment. I'd fall down or faint. I wanted to put my name down for the TV show Expedition Robinson (where competitors have to survive on a desert island for a few weeks). But I had to put down my weight and height. I know that if they were to see it they wouldn't think twice about letting me take part. So, without me even realizing how big an effect my weight could ever have on living a normal life, it's now started to rule my life!

Yesterday I felt as if I'd achieved something, by speaking with Sandra. Today on the other hand, I had a normal breakfast, but I got so hungry, so I had muesli and I wanted to stuff my face. I felt worthless again. That feeling didn't go until I was at work, when my thoughts weren't on my digestive system. That full stomach, how bad I felt! I can kind of imagine how the next period is going to go. On bad days, all I'll want to do is stay inside, not seeing anyone. This has actually happened a few times over the past while, when I just didn't want to see anyone because of looking so bad. Today I felt the same. I then bumped into two familiar faces. It affected my reaction towards them. I wasn't myself. Anyhow, on other days I'll be feeling strong, as if I can do it. You need willpower and determination if you want to get back to normal. And it's so true. But to go twenty-four hours without food, you always need to be devoted and strong.

10-03-08

Yesterday I went to a friend's house. The moment we stepped in the door, it was, 'EAT! Come on Niamh, EAT!!' And every little

*bite I put in my mouth they were watching. It was awful. I had
to stuff myself. I didn't want to. The soup, with massive amounts
of Es, carbs and then white bread. It was starchy and filling and
so fattening. Then the dips on the crackers. Mayonnaise! Yuck,
yuck, yuck. All afternoon it was fatty drinks, cappuccinos and
biscuits. I didn't want to and I felt so bad. The whole afternoon
I knew I needed to try and make room for the big dinner, because
if I didn't eat it, they'd think the worst of me. So when the dinner
came, which was cooked in greasy oils and sauces, I needed to
do everything I could to force it down. I then agreed to eating the
dessert. They said, 'Being the size you are, you can afford to put on
some weight and eat ****.' So what if I can?! It still makes me feel
awful. And it did.*

*The train ride back home was a living hell. I could feel the fats
and oils and sugars and sweets flowing through my veins. It was so
bad. And there was nothing I could do. I had to let my body absorb
it. A moment on the lips (and it wasn't even an enjoyable moment)
is a lifetime on the hips. Those words were going around in my
head, as well as 'you are what you eat'. All I did was stress myself
out about how to get rid of the calories. 'Shall I jog home? Or
shall I take the long way around? Or shall I do yoga tonight and
go jogging or rollerblading in the morning? But then, to do that,
I'd need to have a proper breakfast and I can't eat that much first
thing because of that disgusting vienetta ice-cream!'*

*I have the habit of asking myself, whenever I put food in my
mouth, 'WHY AM I EATING? Is it boredom? Is it hunger? Is it low
energy? Is it for my taste buds?' And the answer to this question has
to be, 'Because I'm hungry and the food is healthy.' But this wasn't
the answer yesterday. Instead it was, 'I'm eating so they won't think
I've got a problem.' Some people should realize how bad they affect
me, by trying to stuff my face. They don't have a clue. And I've had
it. I think I'm going to stop eating with friends. Nobody understands
what it's like. It's a vicious circle. I know I need to work on it. But it's*

not going to vanish overnight. I've brought this problem on myself, so now I need to solve it. But I'm so scared of putting on weight. It terrifies me. I dream about it. You know when you have a nightmare and you wake-up and are so happy that it's over? That's what I've been having so often. Last night in bed, I was so worried. I've been feeling so weak. Will I be able to do the tour-guiding job? It's three months from now… I've got three months of study in my spare time… My focus hasn't been great. I get really weak whenever I have to talk for a longer time. I get lightheaded. What's it going to be like when I'm on the bus, speaking on the microphone (in German!) most of the day and standing in front of forty people? Is it a good idea, or should I just call it all off?

Oh well, I can't think about that too much. Tour-guiding will keep me busy and burning calories. What a disaster though. It isn't fair. I don't know what to do anymore. I'm scared and I need the scales to see what has happened over the past three weeks. But I have to wait two more weeks. All this disgusting eating I've been doing. I need to detox but if anybody finds out, they'll go crazy. I feel so lightheaded, weak and dizzy. My muscles have no strength. So I'll have special K for dinner. Not a lot though and 2.5ltrs of water to flush all the sugar out of my body. Oh my god, what the **** am I playing at! My body needs to be disposed of. Does anybody ever feel such pains in their stomach? Does anybody ever feel so full and bloated? Is there anybody out there who knows what this feeling is like?! I need someone to tell me I'm not alone. I need someone to tell me I'm not insane. Please!

***

I was so aware of my situation. I could see the contradiction that was going on within me. I knew I needed to change, I knew I needed to gain weight. I knew I was lacking energy and that I was struggling. My cousin was somebody special to talk to. She was the first person I actually took advice from, in terms of how to change the eating patterns I'd created. She had the most gentle approach, as we sat at the bar one night, drinking bottles of wine. She didn't pressure me and this gave me strength. She didn't make me feel like a failure for struggling. Those precious few moments, even in a slightly intoxicated state, I felt I could do it. I truly felt I could fix this all by myself. I never spoke the dreaded words of 'eating disorder' or 'anorexia'. I used pretty much the same stories as I'd been using over and over again, when convincing loved-ones of my healthy behaviour. But, something glimmered, when we spoke. An element of my true problem came to light within me and I wanted to take that strength and determination and put it to good use and get myself back on track, without the help or interference of others.

But the tricky part was that I had no clue of what was right or wrong. I didn't know what behaviour was necessary. I wanted to gain, I wanted to loose. I wanted to eat, I wanted to starve. I wanted to achieve, but I was failing. I wanted an easy life, but putting on weight was too painful. I wanted happiness, provided by the perfect weight and reflection. But I was miserable.

My cousin and I parted ways after that revealing chat and I really wanted to fix myself. But the urges to binge uncontrollably were intensifying and making it more fearful to actually eat. It was April by this stage and I'd been having many episodes of binging, since my behaviour got out of hand back in Darwin (nine months previous). The longer I deprived my body, the stronger the urges to binge were becoming. This then encouraged me to fear eating anything at all. The awareness of the binges was the best fuel to strengthen Anna, because not eating (which is what she wanted) didn't provoke the goodness within me. Not eating wasn't teasing the healthy side of me that wanted nutrition. That part of me couldn't be tempted or teased, if it was slowly being trained to forget those temptations ever existed! Feeling hunger was easier than feeding my body. It was a done deal!

Either way, the contradiction was onset and I knew my strength and my willpower. So I was determined to battle it out. I needed isolation in order to do so. But the whole reason for living by Anna's rules was to prove my amazement to the outside world. Now though I feared how others would see me, if my problem would become widespread news. That felt like the failure of a lifetime! I'd always been known as the one who succeeded in life. I was the happy one. I wanted to show others how I indulged in LIFE. However, an indulgence of any kind would never take place—not if a potential binge was on the cards. I would have rather starved, especially in my awareness that I was damaging myself.

I had my busy life, I worked forty hours a week, I kept myself active, I distracted myself from the hunger, I partied and I constantly tried so hard to keep up with the pace of life. I was working towards my travel goals too, which kept me driven. The study that was in preparation of the tours, was a burden and a huge strain due to the lack of brainpower, energy and concentration. I was eager however to pursue. Until one day, a minor hick-up offered me the relief my physical body needed, even though it wasn't supporting dreams of Mexican travels. I received news that the tours had been cancelled. With that, I realized I'd have no extra funds to travel and so, my dreams seemed to fall apart. I was at a loss. Life was happening and I was failing. The light I felt to have found in the darkness (when I first decided to aim for Mexico) had been switched off. I didn't know how to escape the life I'd pushed myself to live in Holland—the one of misery that I deserved but hated so much. There was almost too much going on, especially when realizing that my obsession with food had gone way too far. There was nothing to lift my spirits. I was on a downward spiral and the only thing I had going for me was this strange obsession. I cried for help, in the words that spilled into my black notebook. I needed a way out, but I also needed to cling to what it was that gave me my strength. So the shameful secret I was burdened with continued to rule my life and push me forward. It was the secret battle aimed at fixing my broken heart.

 **6**

APRIL 2008

06-04-08

A lot has happened, food wise, over the past week. Ma's back in Holland for the week, she's just visiting. She spoke to me about food and wanted me to actually come back to Ireland, just to see her doctor. That was the only reason! I thought it was over the top. But that kind of made me realize how worried she must be about me. Now I've been stuffing myself. I can't stop and I feel full, all the time. It's not a great feeling. But I do eat. I just eat consciously. I told Ma the cycle I'm in. I told her I have to eat healthy foods and that I feel yuck when I eat yuck. But I know I need to put on weight. But I don't know how it's ever going to happen, when I'm so strict and cautious about what I put in my mouth!

I feel like people are constantly judging me. They think I'm ill. Just look at the food diary I keep. Isn't that a lot of **** I put in my mouth? I think so! So there isn't a soul that can say I don't eat. People see me eating. Isn't it better to eat yoghurt and fruit for dinner than a plate of chips and greasy ****—which is what most people eat once a week? For them it's a treat. And for me, cereal for dinner is also a treat. It's healthy at the same time. Delicious! I feel in control. I'll go to the doctor here in Holland. I promised Ma. I'll tell him what I told Ma. I'll explain and I'll have a full examination.

08-04-08

*Right, I just had a good dinner. I finished it an hour ago.
I feel nicely full. I feel stronger. I'm not feeling the need to eat
uncontrollably. So this is good! I think. But it did take a lot to
actually decide what to eat. Having the dinner took forever too.
Sometimes it's like there's a barrier. It's as if something is stopping
me from letting myself eat anything other than yoghurt and cereal.
Eating is harder because of this barrier. But whenever I eat with
somebody, I can eat proper portions and I stuff my face, big time.
I stuff my face to the point where I can hardly move. So what's that
all about? When I know someone will be watching me, is that the
only time I can sit down and eat a proper meal? That's so strange!*

*But it's all in my mind. It's all in my head, this barrier. It isn't
physically in my body, my throat or my stomach. It's in my head.
How frustrating. It's not going to disappear. Why not? Because
I need to work on it! Slowly it's become stuck inside my mind and
my life is revolving around it. And that isn't going to go away
overnight. I have to always stay obsessed with food, because if I'm
not obsessed with eating consciously, I'll become a big fat cow.
So how do I beat it? How can I? By admitting to Ma? But I didn't
tell her how it's ruling my life. What I told her was true, but the
extent of the problem, I kept to myself. I'm so ashamed. That's why
I never gave her the whole story. I really don't know why and how
it has come to this point. Hopefully I'll have a small meal—if I get
the chance to eat alone.*

22-04-08

*I just have to let you know. I've had a pasta salad with fresh
vegetables and tuna for dinner. Absolutely gorgeous! I didn't want
to eat it at first. A friend asked me if I wanted some. I wanted
yoghurt and cereal again. But I ate the pasta instead and I feel so*

good. I've had my meal and I'm not eating until tomorrow morning now. I feel satisfied and good about myself. I know how I would have felt if I'd have eaten only the cereal and fruit. I would still want food and if I'd have had some beer, I would have definitely wanted bad food. I feel so strong. I should keep this feeling so close to me. I need to feel this more often. Good good good. What a realization, a revelation and a triumph! Keep you posted on how I feel in the morning (because I didn't want to have a big dinner in the first place, after the biscuit I ate, but I still forced myself and it worked out okay). Good!

***

Repetition, repetition, repetition! I repeat, I repeat and I repeat some more, 'I'm eating', 'I'm not ill' and 'I'm healthy'. These were the precious moments when Anna was strengthening her beliefs and I was being truthful and open in expressing my main thoughts and drive through life. The main thing I could focus on was the repetition of these so-called mantras, just to convince myself I was happy. The principles were only becoming more and more a part of who I felt to be. They were affirmations that would help me to stick to the behaviour I'd been applying. I'd stay as strict as possible, in order to avoid being faced with the fear of putting on weight, which I'd convinced myself was going to happen. The starving was more and more frequent, due to the episodes of binging, all with the purpose of compensating and creating a balance. The binges felt to be a bigger problem. The affirmations I felt I needed, kept me satisfied and I would forever project happiness in every area of the apparently fulfilling life I lived.

I was no longer living to prove to others I was healthy, but I was living to prove to myself that I was healthy, happy and different. The world no longer mattered. What was more important was my distance from that world and my family, so I could continue establishing myself as being a person of some sort. The seal of approval I'd initially hoped to gain from the world, by having returned as the traveller who never gained weight and by being able to live 'normally' in a stable life with a secure job. But gaining that seal from outsiders had slowly become insignificant. Instead I, as a person, needed to be the one who stamped my self with that gold seal, which was the confirmation of being 'good'. I had to earn it though. So I needed to step away from the world, as much as my life would permit, and internalize the search.

The approval I was searching for, I only hoped would appear in the words I wrote. Who was I writing to though? My black notebook was slowly becoming a person, which was a new development. When I first started to spill my thoughts onto paper, back in August 2007, this wasn't the case. Back then, I was the only one who was in control. I wasn't addressing my entries to anybody. Now, there was actually somebody I started devoting my worthy words of thoughts and feelings to. A personality was being introduced and it was the personality I was living for, more and more. It was literally somebody who was judging me, keeping tabs on everything single thing I did in my life and filling me with so many fears of what would become of my reality if I were NOT to do what this certain somebody wanted me to do. I couldn't see this certain somebody, but they were definitely there. The presence I could feel was in the form of the barrier that stood initially between myself and food and slowly was standing between myself and life; the food issues were now my life.

The mental block between myself and life, meant that the outside world was no longer participating. It counted for nothing. I didn't subconsciously choose my loneliness. The choice was unknowingly taken and it was reflected in the words I wrote. I was aware there was a problem and I wanted to fight. No matter what direction I chose—to fight or not to fight—loneliness was the only way forward so as to avoid the irrational fear of being disapproved of by the outside world (when admitting to having a problem) and to avoid the certainty of being disapproved of by my inside world (when choosing to eat).

The mental barrier gave me the ability to force energy into my life, so I could still work and sustain myself and engage with my dear friends. Others were starting to reach out to me. But the block was there and I was closed off to any connection that could go deeper than the skin and bones others saw me slowly becoming but the fat and grease I felt to be. The cries for recognition and for help were only written in moments of despair. These cries were going against the principles I'd been imprinting in my psyche as I practised the affirmations. So there was no way I'd have openly been able to spill my truth, during the moments when either I was trying to reach out to something or someone or when others were trying to reach out to me.

Daily life was still being lived. I was using all of my strength and willpower to function at work, to keep my focus, to maintain the friendships I had and to party as frequently as my body would permit. Everything was now ultimately to hide my truth from my closest friends and family.

7

MAY 2008

10-05-08

I've made an appointment. I'm going to the dietician. I don't know what's going to happen but I know one thing for sure: I can't look at myself in the mirror. The summer has come and people are wearing cool, gorgeous clothes and everyone is looking amazing. I'm looking like ****. My face is awful. I look like a forty-year-old woman. I'm wrinkled, fat and unhealthy. I look ill. When will I be able to look in the mirror and be pleased with what I see? Will I ever be normal again? I doubt it. I look like a ghost, but with a massive head and a fat face. What am I going to do? Will I be able to admit it and talk to someone? Do I need a companion? Do I need someone who is going through the same? Will that make me feel understood? I don't know what's going on. How did it come to this? What happened and where did I go so wrong? How did I go so wrong? I have no clue.

21-05-08

I went to the dietician and she didn't understand me. Nothing! I literally asked her, 'Do you understand?' She said, 'No, not really.' ****! *%%"!! That's what I thought. I thought that between her and the doctor someone would understand me. But no, they didn't. I knew once I was sitting there that I needed a different kind of help. This wasn't going to work. This was totally the wrong approach. The things she was telling me to eat were just making me sick. The

*thoughts alone! There was a feeling of panic. **** ***** ****!
What am I going to do? It made me feel like ****! Oh my god,
how did it get this far and why did I let it get this far? I don't want
to do this anymore. But I don't know where to turn. Who do I turn
to? Nobody understands. It's frustrating, it's scary, it's crazy. I hate
myself. I hate the way I look and what I eat. I hate myself for both
of these reasons. I hate myself for needing food. I don't deserve it.
I feel good when I don't eat. I'm strong. But then I feel yuck once
I do eat because I scoff a load of dirt. And that's worse. Actually
I don't scoff dirt. But whatever I eat, it's loads. It's too much. It's
disgusting. Then there's no break. My brain just keeps on going and
telling me to eat. I'm not listening to my stomach because I could
be full after half a meal but I still keep on eating.*

*After I left the dietician, I really needed to speak to someone
who understands. That's all I needed, just a bit of response. I'm
sick of people looking at me as if I'm crazy because I know there
are so many people out there battling with the same ****, day in
day out. Yesterday I made a slight break through. I actually went
shopping, not for yoghurt and cereal but for vegetables and other
foods—things that will actually make a meal. That was big. And
I bought full fat milk. Really I need full fat yoghurt too but I can't.
All of a sudden, to buy all these awful foods which are high in
calories, without feeling guilty and bad, was a big thing. That
was so good and today I ate loads. I had a small breakfast and a
muesli bar, three slices of bread and a massive pizza. Yesterday
was another good day. But after two good days, I don't want to eat
tomorrow. Can I do it? Can I eat? I'm scared. I don't know what
to do. But then I think it can't all be really as bad as I'm making it
out to be? I'm fine you know. But deep down I know I'm not fine.
What's going to become of me? What will happen if and when I put
on this weight that everyone is forcing me to gain? This is bad,
really bad.*

***

Help, recognition and support, were things I desperately needed. But I couldn't face the shame of actually being open and honest about the fact that I'd made a mess of my life. In those painful moments, I browsed the internet and found websites about eating disorders. I found some contacts in America, which was safely distant. I found some contacts in Holland too, but that was dangerously close. I spilled my heart to a total stranger who lived on the other side of the world who was also suffering, hoping that she would miraculously be someone who could help me. I eagerly waited the reply, but of course it never came! So I browsed the internet, I looked at pictures, videos and documentaries. It gave me a sense of belonging. It showed me that I wasn't alone in the world.

The trip to the doctor and the dietician was an act to hide the real problem from my Mam. In her faraway presence—as my Mam lived in Ireland—she encouraged me to get some help. I was willing to do what she wanted, yet, because she wasn't near, I still was able to continue living as I did. I'd only seen my Mam two times in six months. She could see the deterioration in my physical state but was at a loss as to what to do or what actions to take. Therefore she practised such caution when we spoke of the subject. For me, it was too painful, too soon and too shameful to be open and honest with her. I knew I hadn't yet reached breaking point. There was more damage to be done and it was happening. So to keep her happy and to convince the whole world that I was hiding nothing, I paid both the dietician and the doctor a visit. I had my stories as usual. The only help the dietician offered was an eating plan, just to gain weight. I tried desperately to follow it for a week.

As she handed me this weekly food plan, she was actually handing it to two different people; as soon as it was time to follow this daily food plan, the preparation of the meal was almost out of my hands and I wasn't participating. I was in the middle of two strengths. They were both trying to cook this food, the meal

I knew I needed. I wanted to explode for doing this one seemingly simple thing. I wanted to so badly but I felt my strong exterior desperately trying to hold on. I tried to ignore the eruption and keep myself together, all the while witnessing myself prepare the food. Mantras I knew worked, so I applied them suddenly. As if out of nowhere I knew what to do to break the belief system I had in place. Something more needed to break, just for me to have the ability to sit down and force the food into my mouth. I continued reassuring myself over and over and over again that if I survived the preparation and consumption of just one meal then I'd be able to live happily. Because it was no longer about the food, it was now about life.

This is what had become of my life. Travel was no longer an option and my Mexican dreams were out the window when the tours I'd hoped to be guiding through Ireland, during my three-week break from the job at the travel agency in Holland, were cancelled. This change in circumstances was about to change the course of my life drastically. The flight tickets to Ireland were still open, as was the three-week holiday I had from my job in Holland. So, on the 1st of June, I reluctantly boarded the plane to visit Mam and my youngest sister and brother. For the fact that Mam loved me so much, I was dreading those three weeks intensely. To love a child is to care, to nourish, to protect and to heal. These were things I didn't deserve and I didn't want. I had to resist them and stay strong so as to avoid the pain that could be brought to me, in my Mam's act of giving, sharing and attending to her lost and underweight daughter. Even before arriving in Ireland, I could already feel the pressure she'd apply, in regards to food and weight. I didn't really want to go but I reassured myself that if it would get too much, I'd simply shorten my holiday and fly back to Holland, where my isolation, my muesli and my yoghurt would be waiting for me.

8

JUNE 2008

04-06-08

I can't write or be as open as usual, at the moment. So I've had to do some writing on the computer just in case someone finds this book. That would be tragic. There's no real privacy here in Ireland. But I'm still keeping track of what I'm eating and when. I can't escape that, so ****! I was feeling the pressure big time yesterday at dinner and I was so angry. It just makes me not want to eat at all, so much more. The thick creamy sauces I'm being forced to eat, don't make me want to eat happily either. But I have to switch off to the bad thoughts, or else I'll definitely not be able to eat. And that will totally make Ma angry and suspicious. Not too sure if she's either of these things at the moment. But I can't worry. I want to cook a meal, but that might raise some suspicions as well. I'll keep you posted. Someone's coming.

06-06-08

Pain in my gut, the creams, the sauces, the fats. Everything is saturated and I can't allow anyone to see me looking at the amount of calories because if they do, then I'm weird. I'm not right in the head. But I know what's happening… These fatty foods are to fatten me up. But once I start to feel the pressure then it will only work the other way, and I won't want to eat anything. It's all going to go so wrong, I can assure you of that. At the moment my stomach is in bits. It's so sore. I've got this burning sensation.

Was it the cider? I'm not drinking that again. Back to rose wine I reckon. But then I'll be weird again, or what? I want to do yoga, but it will be the same thing. I'll be obsessed and stupid. But then again, who cares? Why should I care what they think?

At the moment, it's 08.25 in the morning and I'm trying not to run upstairs and stand on the scales. I'm fighting the urge. Can I do it? I don't know. I'm going to try anyhow. I'll try not to stand on it until Sunday morning, depending on what I drink on Saturday night. I'm going to put it off, for as long as possible. I'm allowed to weigh myself once a week. That's normal. Keep you posted on what else they'll be stuffing down me today.

07-06-08

Good day yesterday. Today is going fine. I've been eating proper dinners—big improvement! Nobody even realizes…

I read this story yesterday about a sixty-year-old woman in the States who is anorexic. She's been suffering for twenty years! And she's convinced she'll recover. I can tell her now it's not going to happen. It took her years to realize that she had an illness and this was thirteen years ago. It will end up killing her. And I feel so sorry for her. It made me realize that I don't want this thing to become me. I've heard a lot of stories about it. Some of the things she wrote were so familiar to me. It was scary. For instance, the fact that she loves to watch food programmes and work-out at the same time. She's obsessed… then I must be too…

There are two different thoughts in my head. Both so strong and so powerful, but they're worlds apart. Which thought should I go for? sometimes—for a few moments—I think I can break it. And I'm convinced I can control it and be fine with putting on weight. But then I feel myself wanting to stand on the scales and hoping that it's the same weight as before. I'm obsessed! The last time I stood on the scales, it was Wednesday morning. It's now Saturday. Tomorrow morning it's time. Then I'll check my weight again. I'm only allowed to do this once a week.

I have to go see the doctor on Monday. Sometimes I just want to come clean and tell Mam everything. I want to be honest because it's so stressful trying to make something into something else. Especially when I know full well what's going on. But I'm ashamed and embarrassed. I don't want to admit to my problem. I don't want this to get the better of me. I don't want to admit defeat. Will I feel better if I put on weight? I don't think so. I think I'll be even more disgusted. I think. I don't know. This book was supposed to help me along the way. It's what people told me last summer in Darwin. But nearly a year later and still I'm struggling. And every piece of food that has passed my lips since then, is in this book. I look through it and it disgusts me that so much **** has gone through my body. How did it get this far? How did it get this bad? When did I go too far? Where did I cross the line?

***

Being back in Ireland was torture. I felt so much panic when I was with my family because I was losing control. Others weren't coinciding with the rules I wanted to live by. I still needed to determine the rules by myself and I was starting to fight a losing battle; but I didn't know who I was fighting for.

Suddenly the physical strength I'd usually have, the strength that would keep me busy and nicely distracted from what was going on, was weakening. Before I went to Ireland, I had the perfect means to constantly avoid my truth, which was by working forty hours and socializing. I would never be too reflective and so I never saw that my every act was in the name of avoiding the shameful feeling of hunger and the longing for nutrition. In Ireland, I suddenly had no more distractions. I was forced to stop. Then all I was facing were my fears and my obsessions within a world I was desperate to escape from.

The situation I found myself in, felt to be out of my hands. I was no longer presented with a choice. I was desperately trying only to strengthen Anna's beliefs, by stating how healthy I was and how much I was eating. However, there was another force that didn't wish for starvation, but longed for food and I somehow needed to keep that force alive. For a few months this was something I did with success; I fought both against eating and against starvation. It was easier with everyone at a distance, this was now changing because of where I was. I was with my family, in my home; the only place on earth where people accepted and loved me unconditionally. I was surrounded by love that I didn't want and by comfort that was torturing me. I was conscious of this fact, yet I didn't understand what these two forces wanted from me—hence the reason for me to not have known who I was fighting for. If I'd have known, then there wouldn't have been any illness to speak of! There wouldn't have been any fear, confusion, lies, secrets, isolation or pain. At that stage, understanding wasn't of the essence because it's not the nature of the illness. Instead destruction is the nature. If nature works as it should, then destruction would be the element through which the illness would eventually serve its purpose.

I couldn't take the mental stress of hiding these issues anymore. I couldn't take the pain of what the food was physically doing to me either. I had no clue as to what the term 'emotion' meant. I was numb, I had no feelings and I was disconnected from life. I was terrified of everything and the pressure from outside was starting to feud with the pressure rising on the inside.

The mental and physical body can only endure so much. The mental barrier can only withstand a certain amount of force before it will break down. The mental block was an obstacle and it was intensifying, making life almost unbearable. There was no flow and the barricade was suddenly experienced and felt throughout my whole body and mind. Emotionally, mentally and physically nothing was able to flow. The outside was trying to get in and the inside was trying to get out. I still had to create the life I'd created in my mind. It needed to become a reality. I was still trying to feel how far I could push myself to deterioration, by engaging as much as was humanly possible in that barrier of unlimited hatred towards myself and life.

One afternoon, I took a time-out and went to the sea in my hometown of Arklow. Those hours cleared the way for the reality of my situation to be brought home. I knew then that I couldn't continue living as I was. I was seeing myself and the mess I'd made, as I suddenly paused to reflect on the race I felt to be running, which was still my life. My day at the sea revealed that I needed to tell someone. So I decided I was going to tell Mam about this strange food obsession. Once upon a time I'd been so sure I'd never speak the words that had been jotted down in my black notebook! However, on that particular day, the writing I did, as I sat on the sand and gazed at the waves, actually gave me the strength and courage to say what I needed and it opened up the door to reveal a part of me I never wanted to expose. A heart-to-heart with my Mam followed my reflective day. During that talk, I didn't actually give myself a label, but instead I made inclinations of my own rising truth. Finally Mam felt she'd been given permission to take matters into her own hands, while I was left to continue as I'd been living.

The destructive force of Anna knew her presence would soon be recognized and would no longer be welcome. For this reason she took control, like never before. Within a few days, her strengthening was almost mind-blowing. The smallest things

I once classed as normal behaviour were suddenly extreme. I hated everything I felt, everything I thought and everything I did. In the smallest of acts, such as checking the calories and doing yoga and standing on the scales, I felt like a loser. These acts were normal things I did and they had been how I managed to get myself through everyday. In Ireland though, I felt I was being observed with every single step I took and every bite I ate. I even felt as though my thoughts were being observed and my words were being monitored. Nothing was 'right' by the observer. Who was this observer? It was Anna. She was becoming evermore present as the time of her revelation came nearer. She was no longer only inside my head, but I saw her in everything and everyone.

The visit to the family doctor was nearing. I felt as though I was awaiting trial. I was going to be convicted for the crime I'd committed. I was going to court and I would be either sentenced to death or I'd be granted my freedom. Subconsciously there were two judges. One judge was weak in presence and held no real exterior but would offer me the guidance back to full health. However it had no power, no clear motives, no statement, no grounds on which to base the truth and no evidence to prove there was innocence. The other judge was strong in presence, with the projection of energy and life. It would offer me the guidance away from the healthy life others were worthy of living, yet I wasn't. I deserved nothing and that's where the stronger judge wanted to take me: towards the nothingness. That was the place where the world reflected exactly what I was: nothing. To feel to be nothing is to live out the desire of becoming nothing. So I prepared for my judgement date and I awaited my sentencing. It was now out of my hands.

9

JUNE 2008

12-06-08

Well, it's all come to a head. It's exploded. It was bound to happen.
Better sooner than later. I went to the doctor on Monday (the 9th)
and I knew when I was sitting in the waiting room that the time had
come—it was time to be honest and admit to my problem. I was so
scared. My heart was pounding and I just wanted to run. I walked
into her office and I burst into tears. I couldn't contain myself.
I found myself making excuses. I was lying and saying that I AM
eating. Because I do! But it goes so much deeper than that. It's not
black and white. That's what a lot of people think.

The doctor weighed me. I'm 34kgs. I thought I was 35.

I felt like a little child as I sat there. My head hung in shame and
all I could do was cry. I wasn't able to admit to the exact problem.
It was so so so so hard. But the doctor, Siobhan, she knew what
was going on. She knew there was more to it. She made me say it.
She made me admit to it. And I did. It took so much for me to do
this. But I did it. I hung my head in shame, I stared at the ground,
I dug deeper than ever before, I had visions of my Da… I stepped
outside of my body and the words came from mouth, stating, 'I'm
anorexic.' Then Ma said I deserved a hug.

Suddenly it all became real. I was hearing serious talk around
me … about somebody who was ill! They were talking about
me???!!! They were discussing how to get it treated and what I'd

*need to do. The consequences I'm facing are huge! The doctor said
I would need to stay in Ireland. By being alone in Holland I won't
recover. I'll just get back into my own routine. She said all the
right things. Or the things that made sense. They were exactly what
I needed to hear, all for me to realize how serious this problem is.*

*I often think it's not all that bad and I'm convinced I can make
myself better. But that's not going to work or else I would have done
something about it six months ago. And I didn't. 'You need people
around you', she said. I knew she was right. But I was saying, 'I need
to go back to work on the 23rd of this month, so I can't stay. I have my
life.' Her answer to this was, 'You have an illness, you need treatment
and therapy and you need to be taken in to hospital!' What!!!!
Hospital! That's so over the top. I didn't say that of course, but
I thought it. She told me to think about what I wanted to do from this
point onwards and I was told to come back on Wednesday afternoon.*

*Oh my god! I can't believe how dramatic these changes are
going to be. I can't believe I have this illness. She's calling it
an illness, an addiction, a disease. It's in the genes, she says.
Maybe that's why my Da came to mind when I was admitting to
my problem. I was in a daze. It was like I wasn't experiencing
anything. I couldn't be. I'm strong, bubbly, sociable and likeable.
Or was that the person I used to be, before this illness took over
my life? The doctor, she asked me if I was depressed, lonely,
happy? I told her I'm happy, as the tears were running down my
face. She asked me, if I was crying tears of joy at that moment?
I remained silent...*

*As I left Siobhan's office, she told me, 'Niamh, you can take the
easy way out or the right way. Which gene do you want to use?'
Well, putting the question like that, the answer was pretty clear.
Even before I left the office, I knew what I needed to do, regardless
if I wanted to or not.*

Afterwards, I needed a strong drink! Mam and I went to a local hotel, where we sat in the bar. I cried a lot. At first I couldn't speak. I wanted to say so much but I didn't know where to start. Slowly I opened up and admitted to certain things. Then I took a major step. I showed Mam my little black notebook. I showed her YOU. I couldn't believe it! I was so shocked for showing her and Mam was even more shocked to actually see YOU and said it was the saddest thing she had ever seen… I was embarrassed and ashamed. How had it come this far? There was just so much to say and so much to deal with and so much to take in. Oh my god! What am I going to do? We then went home and I was going to wait until I'd made my decision before coming clean to my brother Sean and sister Eileen about the whole illness. I had a huge amount of thinking to do. I was panicking about how it was all going to plan out. I would need to tell everyone. There was so much practical stuff to think about too. I was terrified most of all about recovering. That night, I wondered, if I was experiencing any of this! Did this dreaded day happen?

Monday the 9th of June 2008. Did it ever take place? Was that me? I reckon so. It's just so surreal. I can't even begin to explain. The next day, I was thinking, thinking, thinking. The whole day was another blur, another daze. It was an out-of-body experience. I walked around town, doing some bits and pieces. Then I was at home, listening to some music, playing cards, reading my book and I then had dinner (noodles without the turkey. I left the meat on the plate). Then Mam asked me if I'd made my decision. And I then said, 'Yes, I'm going to stay.' That deserved another hug. Mam was relieved and this step shows that I do want to get better.

18-06-08

Monday I was thinking about being stuck here in Ireland with no friends, for months on end. What am I going to do? Everything is so uncertain and that's what gets to me the most. I don't know what treatment there'll be. We're going to Holland for a week, in the next few days. I'll have to tell everyone about this thing. It will be torture.

I can feel the rage inside of me building up as I'm thinking about getting help and choosing to stay in Ireland and leaving my life behind in Holland. So I have to avoid thinking about anything. I'm not going to focus on the negatives or else I'm just giving myself more grief and stress. And it's all unnecessary. I'm not doing it. I've been putting off telling some of my closest friends back in Holland. I really don't want to. I don't want people to label me. I don't want people to look at me differently. Because I still am the same person. I'm going to email them today. It has to be done. These are all the little steps I must take. But I'll get there in the end. Keep you posted. Greetings from a fat *****.

***

The day I went to the doctor's office was a day I'll never forget. Everything I'd come to value in life was suddenly turning against me. The shame filled every fibre of my being for all that I'd created. But I still smiled. I still believed I was happy even though I didn't know the true meaning of the word. I wished to go about life in the same manner as before. But there was no way that would have worked, for the simple fact that my Mam was living in Ireland and I was living in Holland. So I was forced to turn my whole life upside down and was given the choice to either stay in Ireland so I could get the help I needed or to return to Holland where I had my life waiting for me. It felt to be one of the biggest decisions I'd ever make in my life. I didn't want to be in Ireland and I felt that by simply having owned up to the crime I felt I'd committed, I was cured and I needed to continue living. Nothing felt to have changed. Just by being diagnosed with anorexia, from one minute to the next, didn't mean I was suddenly at death's door. That's where a part of me wanted to be, as I reluctantly chose to stay in a country that didn't make me happy and fight an illness I knew I'd been diagnosed with but didn't feel to have—not to any extremes.

When making my decision, what came to me was the strength I'd slowly been giving life to, as I wrote in my black notebook— the strength that wanted to break away from these bad habits during the previous six months. It was that same entity of existence that came from that deeper source, when taking the courage to speak the words I thought would remain unspoken forever—the truth of being anorexic. It was the source of life I needed. It told me I couldn't run and hide anymore and that I needed to face the consequences and take full responsibility for my life.

These were still such early days. Anna had been revealed and with this revelation she knew she would soon be evicted. There was no reason for me to disguise my restrictive behaviour. I didn't need to tell anymore lies nor did I need to overly consume food. It was time for Anna to do as much damage as possible—as the outside world took action to conspire against her.

My amazing Mam sought help. Medical consultants were approached and I continuously stayed in the surroundings of comfort and love. Anna didn't want any of this and that urge to resist any kind of help, got stronger. So my food consumption became less, my body became weaker and my barriers strengthened, with each week that passed. Help wasn't yet at hand, the villain was still within and it still needed to reach its fullest potential, which it hadn't yet done. So deterioration was the only way forward! I continued to practise the behaviour, only more extremely, as I felt there was nothing really left to live for, except for one last week in Holland. We were planning on going back for a week for the christening of my sweet little niece. This was still in the month of June, around the same time as 'coming out the closet'. It was also the week when I'd be telling my friends. This was such a positive step, no matter how hard it was. By owning up I was letting myself still feel to have some sort of connection with them, no matter how distant I was to become. I also still needed to have the certainty that I was recognized as being the friend, the energy, the life and the soul. Even with the label I'd been given, I still appeared to thrive on the projection of being happy, bubbly and invincible. So all was still well!

JULY 2008

03-07-08

Oh my god, what's been happening these past weeks? It's been an emotional rollercoaster ride and for some reason eating has become even harder and I don't know why. The binge happened on Friday. Afterwards, on Saturday morning, I was livid. I sat in Emma's kitchen crying because I ate the big bowl of muesli. But I didn't feel to be experiencing it... I felt miserable. So I walked into town. But ended up walking for two-and-a-half hours just to burn the muesli. My weight has gone up a kilo. I'm now 35kgs. I was 35.2 instead of 34.2! This made me go crazy. When I was walking around in a daze, I was scared for the christening; it was happening that same afternoon. I knew I'd be confronted with close family and friends. I'd need to explain myself. I should've been excited but I was terrified. I was obsessively walking and thinking about the bowl of muesli, with all the sugars.

During that two-and-a-half hour walk, it was just me and my music. That's all that existed in the world. It's so strange. If my legs would have allowed it, I would have been jogging. But they would have given way from underneath me I think. Then I had to come back down to earth. I had to switch my thoughts back to normal life. I stopped walking and got myself ready. I tried to look my best and put on my happy face. It worked. I avoided talking to people I didn't feel comfortable with. I didn't want to answer questions about my life. I didn't want to have to explain myself. It's nobody's business. So everything went fine. But I was drinking too much rose wine! And I got myself into that vicious vindictive cycle...

I've told most of my friends and met some close people before leaving for Ireland again. Everyone has been so supportive. I knew that not everyone would react the way I wanted. Everyone deals differently with people in need of support. I just need to focus on myself. I'm glad I told them all now. I've been honest and I'm willing to talk and keep them up-to-date. All the support I've already received has been amazing. I couldn't ask for more caring friends than the ones I've got. I know I'm blessed by them and my family. I couldn't have 'come out' without them. And most of all, it's down to my Mam. This is only the start. I've still got this mountain to climb.

I've decided to quit alcohol for the time being. It's wrecking my body and my head and making my moods worse. It's no good at all. I spoke to Mam about it and she advised me to quit. I know she's right. So Saturday night was my last alcohol binge. I don't know how long for. But for now, it's done. I'm afraid though.

My weight has to stay the same. It's been nearly four weeks since I first admitted to my problem. And I'm still doing the same. I'm still obsessing and feeling fat and I still don't want to indulge. It just goes to show how easy one week rolls into the next, without anything happening. Things just carry on. But I hope that from next week, things will start to happen. Even if it's counselling.

Part III

 **1**

JULY 2008

From the first week in July, I was back in Ireland for an
unforeseeable amount of time. A new chapter had started, all for
the good of my health. I was living with my Mam, my youngest
sister Eileen and only brother Sean. It was now clear to all
what was going on. But what wasn't clear, was how I would get
treatment. As we waited for a miracle to happen and for help to
come our way, the illness was spiralling out of control. I had no
grip on my thoughts, my feelings, my behaviour, my body, my
surrounding world, my life. I had no control over what treatment
was being sought and life was starting to happen around me.
I was here but I wasn't taking part. I was caring less and less
about living. My Mam was the one who was thrown into an
unknown world of eating disorders, where she was left to find
help in addition to what the medical system was offering—
which was merely one hospital appointment for a simple
assessment, that wouldn't take place until six weeks later.

Something told me to take any help I could get, so I could
get my life back on track. It was the voice that told me there
was something left to live for. It told me there was more to life
than the illness and the world was waiting! It was the voice
that brought me to the sea in Arklow so I could face what was
becoming my reality. It was the voice that spoke the words of
my truth to my family, friends and the family doctor. Every
single thing these silent whispers were telling me, was somehow

coming through—even though my five senses were gradually numbing. However, the destructive voice of Anna was suddenly finding Ireland to be a place where punishment had the perfect outlet—for as long as the search for treatment lasted.

Throughout the month of June and into July, my Mam searched for help, through all lines of communication. In the meantime, as I hastily walked and desperately tried to loose non-existing weight to preferably loose my life, I found myself surrounded more and more by darkness. And Anna's voice was now blaring in my ears and spilling from my mouth, 'I'm fine, there's nothing wrong with me'. This provided her more strength. She was now all-consuming my life and ill-consuming food.

Secret desires

My favourite foods
nobody has a clue

Nuts muesli sushi
until I could spew

Freshly baked bread
toasted with melted cheese

The smell waters my mouth
but no fat please

Chocolate has to be dark
to get the ultimate taste

Maybe I'd like an Indian
with a spicy paste

Can I give in?
Not in a million years
To do so
would bring me to floods of tears

Why would I put myself through such emotional pain?
This is an unanswered question that will forever remain...

***

Slowly, writing started to take on a different course. The black notebook no longer felt to be offering me the relief I needed. There was simply too much going on. There was a pull from the outside world that I wanted to sustain. I may have been suddenly ill, but I wanted to be a part of life, so desperately.

When my family and friends found out what was happening, I felt their support intensely. I felt I was able to be honest about my feelings, my thoughts and this whole journey. I wasn't being judged and they still loved me, regardless of the sense of hatred, failure and loathe I had towards myself. I cherished these relationships so much. This is why I felt like I owed them more than what I was giving at that stage of my life, as I was literally giving them nothing but heartache. To me, my existence felt to be overbearing, but they never once turned away from me. The only thing I had to offer—as my world was closing down around me—was my appreciation for their love. I could only express this by keeping them updated on what was going on in my world. And so, from July onwards, everything I wanted to share with them, I put in writing. I posted the updates online, on a self-created blog, which friends and family, in both Holland and Ireland (as well as Australia and America), could access.

I needed the blog in order to keep the connection I had with them as strong as possible. I had no clue of the journey that was in front of me. Nor did I suspect that this urge to keep the lines of communication open and flowing, was to be in aid of my own recovery. Life didn't feel all too bad when I knew there were people out there who were following my words and supporting me from a far throughout my recovery. They were never criticizing or judging me for having 'failed'. I felt less alone. And so, from the 5th of July, I stepped away from hiding my secrets in my black notebook as I moved towards the world by becoming an open book, for everyone to read. There wasn't a day that went by, not a feeling left to linger nor a realization left unrecorded, throughout months of battling that followed. The blog became an accumulation of approximately half a million words in the form of ranting, analyzing, wondering, worrying, loving and rhyming. It was the source of my inspiration and my healing.

In order for the blog to have taken on a life of its own, I somehow was able to let go of my proud exterior as well as the shame that I felt and instead I gained an inner strength for choosing to express who I was, in each and every moment. I switched off to all the voices in my head, that were telling me I was going too far in my expressive choice of words. I ignored the fact that being so truthful could have caused grief and heartache to those I love so much, as they were reading of my inner struggle. I was inconsiderate in a way and often felt it was a selfish act: spilling without thinking of the consequences.

However, my support system had been set in place, with this step. And the blog actually brought certain people into my life who chose, out of the goodness of their heart, to offer me more guidance than I ever felt I deserved, nor ever expected. There's one person in particular I'm referring to: my cousin Mark. What an amazing rock he turned out to be!

My choice to write kept my nearest and dearest, as close as possible. It offered them understanding for what was going on, which would benefit the interactions and levels of communication, both throughout the process of healing as well as future relating. The blog became a form of life that can only be classed as a recording of a once in a lifetime journey through the body, mind and soul. The intense gratitude for this additional healing method only came much later. At the time I was still very much oblivious to the deeper meaning of what I was creating.

A wee poem

Why does life take certain twists and turns?
To make us stronger or for our souls to burn?
Is it fair that some are blessed and others have pain?
Is the balance unequal or is it all fair game?

Is there a reason
I hear myself ask
To overcome certain impossible tasks

It's all just a test that we can pass or fail
And we then sink or swim
after our strength is unveiled

***

The four week search for alternative treatment was suddenly concluded only two days after I'd set up my blog. It wasn't a moment too soon either, because as time was suddenly running out, so was my weight. The messages my Mam sent out into the airwaves, as a cry for help, were answered. Forces of the world brought an amazingly special lady into my life and it was due to my Mam's persistence that the avenue of therapy opened itself up to me. The result was a one-hour session every week, for as long as recovery would last.

My first appointment was on the 7th of July. What I recall from the first few encounters with this amazing lady, who goes by the name of Diann, is, to this day, still very little. All I remember is that she sat in front of me and held something so special. What was it that she was holding in her hands? She held life within her hands. It was overwhelming to be offered so much, after I'd taken it all away, leaving myself empty of love and seeping with shame, self-loathe and disgust. She was such a source of life, light and beauty. But Anna was getting stronger and my ignorance to what was going on, was taking over any feelings I'd been having of wanting to recover. I didn't understand why I had the illness, I didn't understand the danger, I didn't feel treatment was necessary and I didn't realize the changes I would need to make.

Whilst sitting in front of somebody so eager to battle my demon inside, a natural response was for this demon to push me further towards deterioration. Diann sat in favour of the whispering inner spirit that guided me and wished for me to live. This subtle force was going against the destruction inside. Diann was there, just like my Mam, just like all of my other family and friends, to conspire against Anna. Diann was a representation of the spirit I felt I'd lost, whilst Anna continued spilling words from my mouth, shouting lies in my ears and closing off my throat so starvation would be pursued.

The help from outside of myself was in aid of my own true soul and spirit. It was to strengthen what I felt had vanished. Everyone was on the side of the person who they loved, they cherished and they willed to live. Nobody was fighting for Anna to live, because Anna didn't mean life. Anna meant death. Everyone was pushing for me realize my own truth. And at that moment, my truth was: I had an illness, I needed to live and I needed to fight. The people around me were pushing the demon to reach breaking point. Anna would only push for so long. And how long was that? For a long as my body would withstand starvation and my organs would function without sufficient nutrition before closing down.

My body being as strong as it was, didn't feel to have suffered enough. So my denial of being ill and my statement, 'I'm feeling fine', accompanied by heartless fake smiles to the outside world, were still my strength and determination. It continued for the remainder of the month July and into the beginning of August.

Please take over

How far can I take it
When do I draw the line

It's worse than I'd like to admit
For my body and soul
There's no more shine

It takes ahold of me so tight

The strength is overbearing
For so long
there's no reason to fight

The illness has taken over
I've stopped caring

***

The first step in the recovery process, once help was at hand, was for me to realize that I was ill. Not until that fact was established within myself, would I be able to fully fight the force at work. My physical condition first needed to be brought to my awareness. I had no clue of the state I was in. I had a mental block that kept me eyes closed when it came to the truth. I had been convincing myself for so long that I was invincible, indestructible, fat and ugly. I believed this so strongly, even if the kilos were now dropping with or without my willingness and conscious participation. I felt I was piling on the weight with every small bite of food I ate, even though my BMI (which is the abbreviation of Body Mass Index, and it's an indication as to how healthy the body weight is, in regards to the height) was in the category of 'severe anorexic' at this stage. So strongly I believed that I didn't need food, I didn't need hospital admittance or any extra help.

Hospital treatment wasn't on hand, not in the manner that was desired whilst dealing with eating disorders. So the uncertainty that I'd be strong enough to break through the barrier and accept the truth, was a factor of fear for those around me, but not for myself. I didn't fear anything really. Only eating. Seeing as though I didn't feel I needed food, I didn't want it nor did I deserve it, then there was nothing to fear! So I was still feeling fine!

During the first sessions Diann gave me clarity and strength and I felt comfort with her. This is what my Mam used as her guarantee that the daughter she'd always known as being strong-willed and determined, would eventually break through the barricade of denial and start fighting no matter how long it would take or what the road of recovery would face her with. Mam believed that therapy was the best way to go, regardless of what those around her were saying. She knew of my powerful spirit and steered and accompanied me down the road I was destined to take: the road towards full health. Attending weekly sessions meant I was accepting the treatment, no matter how little I initially believed I was ill. I was returning, week after week, and willingly yet begrudgingly listening to and speaking of a person who I didn't feel in any way connected to. I listened and I spoke; I denied and I confessed; I raged and I revealed, up until the point came when I finally crumbled and accepted that I was that person and I did have that illness.

The approach Diann took when bringing the reality of my situation home, was something of an art form only the personally experienced and unique individual would know how to apply, when approaching somebody who was slowly approaching death by the power of their own mind. She eagerly drilled through my mental block, by using words of truth and by never judging me as being bad or dishonest for what I'd created in my life or for whatever words were spilling from my mouth. In the early days, she focused on my current state of being and stressed the importance of entering into the present situation and accepting what life was presenting me with. She willed for me to realize I wasn't fine, I wasn't healthy, I didn't need to smile when I wasn't happy and my strength and determination didn't need to be used in order to self-destruct. Diann's goal was initially to keep me out of hospital. And she did so, by using such gentleness when connecting with me and forming a base so we could both fight for the same thing: my life. She used such sincere concern and honesty in the harsh reality of what could happen if I continued to live in the same manner as I'd been living, throughout the years gone by. She used such patience as I spilled my anger for being in Ireland, my hatred towards food and my desperation to travel. She picked up on my inner passion and knew, for some reason, what it was in life I needed so as to see the truth of the illness. Those were the keys she used. It was truly amazing. In those first weeks—even in my daze, delirium, oblivion, ignorance and stubborn self—she, a stranger to me and my life, saw what not all strangers would've seen. Others would've seen a skeletal figure and a sad lonely soul. She saw there was so much more underneath it all.

I can now see, on hindsight, due to the fact that she recognized something deep within me, I recognized something deep within her and a connection was in place. Gradually the base she'd created meant our bond grew. With time it appeared that when she spoke, I was the student, she was the teacher; I was the sponge, she was the water; I was the reader, she was the book. It was like being transported to another place, where everything she said, was exactly as it was meant to be. Throughout the months that followed I never questioned her words and she was to become my source of inspiration, information and my main system of support. She was to become the only ears in the whole world that were allowed to listen to the disgusting thoughts that kept me awake during the hours of the night and forced me to sleep during the hours of the day. During those first weeks we somehow established the relationship that was needed, in order for us to work on rebuilding my body, mind and soul.

What to do?

Everyday
all day long
Resisting food makes me strong

Do I act on a feeling of hunger or control
The answer to this will determine my goal

Do I want to be skinny and suffer great loss
Or do I want to live life as fully as poss

I've made the wrong choice along the way
And not yet achieved my ultimate body decay

But realizing at this stage
doesn't mean it's too late
So I hope to feel the hunger
and take a leap of fate

***

Taking into account how I've travelled, planned, set goals, needed approval through achievement and never let myself drop out of the race—which I still considered to be my life—meant my body needed to become practically non-existent so I would stop and heal myself. If I wouldn't have broken my body down to such an extent, where my BMI was 13.5 and at high risk of developing osteoporosis and experiencing kidney failure, brain shrinkage, muscle deterioration, heart strain and digestive problems—all the signs I needed telling me my body was choosing to give up—then I never willingly would have dropped out of the race and would never have faced the world as being the failing and incompetent non-achiever that didn't deserve to walk upon this earth. The physical breakdown went hand-in-hand with something to be considered a mental breakdown—or an all-round burnout.

Body and mind work so closely together and the body cannot become almost non-existent without the mind being affected, not when it was initially due to the power of the mind that my body was breaking down. So I was at a stage where the body needed to nearly stop functioning for the realization to come to light, that the burnout was caused by issues of the mind.

Both the game of life and the race were coming to a halt. I was trapped in a body that wasn't able to partake. It needed nutrition, rest, attention and love. But my mind wasn't too eager to give this to my body. My mind was the strong believer that I wasn't worthy of food, of rest, of love and of life. Yet my physical condition was the blessing disguised in my hatred towards myself. My body forced me to rebuild IT, if there was any desire at all to still remain a part of this physical world. This fact alone, made me see how my behaviour had brought me to such a dark place. It made me see that I was living according to principles that were never going to give me the life I wanted. Breaking down made me grasp the fact that I needed to drastically change my ways. I slowly needed to accept that my values in life weren't based on my truth but instead on the lie that I wasn't deserving of anything if I wasn't achieving, proving and running around the world. These latter values actually ended up robbing me of my values! Such a contradiction is what I was experiencing. I found that I valued achievement, energy, independence, approval, health, work, travel, confidence and dreams. But by living according to these values, I was without achievement, energy, independence, approval, health, work, travel, confidence and dreams. To see this inner conflict, showed me I really was living a lie.

Fated Misery

Is it destiny that bad things will challenge us?
Is there really a need for us to deal with the fuss?

There will only be a reason
if we take it on and turn it around
Or else the **** is still there
lying on the ground

Should we just deal with it as best we can?
Or ignore it and hope the **** will never hit the fan?

The easiest answer is to run and hide
The wisest one is to take it in our stride

But as we do
Where do we find the inner strength?

Will we push it to unbelievable lengths?
Without it
challenges are far more daring

So we must
find it
use it
and then start caring

***

I needed to pass through the stage of breaking down my body and mind so I could get to a place within myself where the work could be done, where the issues could be faced and where recovery could commence. Even whilst still being controlled by Anna, I had this yearning to learn and grow and benefit from an illness that held its source so deep and had become visible to the world, as I was merely skin and bone. The illness had started on the inside and worked its way through my whole being. From my depths it had passed through my mind and had become the physical manifestation in the world. This meant I had to reach back into that place where the illness held its source. It was the only place where healing could be found and so the cycle almost needed to be reversed. The journey needed to be turned back on itself with the help of my physical body that had crumbled.

The barricades that were firmly in place were so reluctant to come down, so early in the game. I was still being controlled by Anna. I had no feelings, no emotion and no mental clarity to see how I needed to fight. The tiny whispering voice inside that had gently pushed me to accept therapy, knew what had to happen for me to reach the point where I would fully engage and learn as much as I desired. That tiny source within, gave way to Anna, and it had the intention of showing me the vastness between both the light and dark side of existence. She willed for me to first face my ultimate fear. And this was only done by following Anna to the place ANNA wanted me to be.

The ultimate fear in life is death, and it wasn't until death suddenly became my vision, that I realized I was ill and I needed to fully embrace every single aspect of what fighting the eating disorder entailed. I slowly approached that door, weeks after my first therapy session.

I reached breaking point after a few incidents occurred. First it was an insight that came to me as I stepped into bed one night.

I suddenly felt how much easier it would be to give in and never to eat again. This is how painfully ashamed I felt for the fact that I had a heart that was ticking. I understood how sufferers would choose death over life. This was followed by the fear I had of my heart slowing down and failing in the middle of the night as I slept. Shortly afterwards I had a dream that I recall so strongly still to this day—a dream that was telling me loud and clear that I'd pushed the illness far enough, I'd lost enough weight (in my 31kgs) and I'd damaged my self to the extremes. The fearless self I promoted myself as being, finally feared death. Yes, this is what I needed! Yes, it's what the illness was in aid of! Both the destructive force and the source of light, needed to experience this.

It wasn't like suddenly the road became clear. It actually meant I was seeing the harsh reality clearly and it was only darkness. With every week that passed, throughout the process of acceptance, and with every step I knew I needed to take for the benefit of my health, the world was becoming darker. I needed to succeed in my acceptance so I could get the job done! I forced and forced and eventually with that succession, I was at the darkest stage of recovery. I was in a place I never before had been.

There are only two extremes of emotions in life: love and fear. Love is the fuel for life. Love has no limits and love will always be the guide that will offer happiness. Fear is limited. It can be felt on many different levels—just like love. But there can come a point in life, when the fear is faced so intensely, that it's either 'do or die'. That limit is breaking point and for many a lost soul it can be the reason to wish for death, especially when feeling there's nothing left to live for. Either 'do or die', 'sink or swim', 'fight or flight'. The limit of fear is found when knocking on death's door. To open that door, either by chance or by choice, is stepping into another world. Did I step into another world, during those weeks of acceptance, when I was terrified to close my eyes, to put food in my mouth and to lose and gain weight all at the same time? Yes, I stepped into another world and a door opened itself up to me. It wasn't death's door. It wasn't the desired door Anna longed for me to open. How close I came to opening it, nobody will ever know, which is insignificant. Either way, Anna brought me there but it was another source that let me open the door to what I now call my soul. I knew I needed to totally embrace the strongest force that guided me there in the first place—being the illness. I needed to start embracing the subtle force that stopped me from opening death's door, which was that subtle whispering force, the source of light and energy that was buried so deeply within my weak heart. Before I could properly embrace that source of light, I first had to embrace that source of darkness.

Upon opening this door, I tried to accept the situation as much as I could. And with that, the speed of recovery was all in my own hands. I realize though, that yes, it was very much due to my own strength that I got to where I needed to be, but I can't take all the credit. It was also very much down to those outside of myself—in particular Diann, Mam and my cousin Mark. It was as if these people were pushing me towards that door and willing for me to open it, so I could endure but recover at the same time! I was suffering for my own benefit, because recovery represented in my eyes pain, struggle, failure, shame, and eating. To others my suffering meant I was choosing life. By embracing the darkness and closing myself off and dealing with the truth, the most amazing plot was unravelling.

The door was shut tightly. And it was where healing could take place. So eager I was to find out who had opened this door and who it was that sat behind it. With this shift in consciousness, an all-important aspect needed to be established. It was the fact that I had the presence of two energies within. As I moved from being in a state of denial towards being in a state of acceptance, I had

to break away from identification with the illness. It turned out
that this was the reason for me to have constantly been speaking
words that sounded like nonsense to others—but truth to myself –
of being 'fine' and 'healthy'. These words were the sign of being
controlled by that powerful force and it felt to be me. But it was the
illness speaking. The illness was saying, 'I'm fine!' Which it was
of course! Having an illness means to suffer. I had an illness and
I was suffering so the illness was speaking to me and telling me,
'I'm fine, I'm a disease and I'm here for the world to acknowledge,
so there's nothing wrong!!!' Like magic!

The split personas were the two energies I'd identified many
months ago, in the early stages of the development. Back then,
I had no understanding that I was seriously developing an eating
disorder, even though I could feel an extra presence entering my
life. I was ignorant to the power of the mind. So I chose to ignore
the knowledge that came to me throughout my moments of truthful
writing. Now however, the illness felt to be me. I had, just like the
majority of the world, always labelled those with eating disorders:
it was who they were and would always be! How hypocritical
I now felt, as I had become the illness I once judged and labelled.

Distancing myself from the disorder was a big adaptation as my
behaviour had solely been fuelled by the illness. So how would
I ever be able to tell the difference between two energies? Wasn't
there only one energy for which I chose to live? No, there wasn't.
I'd already encountered more, even at this early stage of recovery.
I'd already felt a source of strength from within. It was the gentle
source of light. That's what I'd chosen to live for. That's what
I was willing to eventually embrace, once my darkness had shown
me all the lessons I willed myself to learn. Those moments of
having something extra, in addition to Anna's power, were only
brief. Such fleeting encounters I'd had; they were gone within
seconds and yet they were just as precious as the air I needed to

breathe. That source was my life. I didn't know where that source had come from and didn't know how I could access it! So how could I identify myself with it? This would actually become the purpose of recovery: finding that source, feeding it, freeing it, and being it! This additional source needed a name. As much as I was against the application of labels, I was advised to use one. And so the extra light—that was still ever so dim—was christened Fay. The reason for me to have chosen this particular name was, just like its origins, at that very early stage of recovery, a mystery. And a mystery it still remains, even to this very day.

The log in the river

Life follows the course of a river
We're all people living our lives, safely on the bank
Events that challenge us
Are gushing by
With so much power and force

Suddenly the bank breaks
I have fallen into the river
I have grabbed hold of a log…

This is safe
This is Anna

My family and friends are on the other side
They are wanting to help me
I want to reach out
And therefore I must let go of the log

Time and time again they call out
I am terrified of letting go
Because I cannot fight the force of the river
I might drown

What will happen if I don't let go?
I will stay forever distant
Distant and isolated from my family, friends and my life

But safe with Anna

I have to challenge myself to take the risk
I have to leave Anna, my log
I have to push across the river

I have to take their hands
I have to put my trust in those who love me
I have to be brave and believe that I will survive

I am therefore reaching
I will struggle
I will make it
I will grab hold
I won't let go

Anna
the log
will be broken by the force of the river
She will be swept away

I will be safe
I will know then
that surviving the river
I will survive anything

***

 **2**

AUGUST 2008

Alongside the safe and secure therapy sessions I was having with Diann there was some extra help being sought and I needed to accept it. This was a huge step because I didn't feel more help was necessary. However my Mam was on a roll and she was willing to give me everything I needed and so much more, to ease my pain. She searched and found an additional form of alternative treatment: acupuncture. She hoped this would offer me some relief and extra guidance—these weren't my hopes however, since I was happy to resist.

When it was first suggested to me, I agreed. But I didn't know what this treatment would involve or what goodness it could offer me. It was also too painful to think I'd be choosing to nourish myself more than I already had been doing, in my sessions with Diann. There was almost too much going on and I wasn't able to process this extra step. I instead let my Mam do what she felt was right for me. So the appointment was made and I was 'off to see the Wizard'!

A wizard is what my acupuncturist, who goes by the name of Ralph, turned out to be. He exceeded my expectations—which were actually non-existent before entering his office (taking into account the frame of mind I was in). My ignorance to the depth of his abilities only meant I was also ignorant to what this treatment involved. I figured it was simply a procedure involving some needles and some body parts. I didn't think there was any participation required from the person who was actually attached to

that body! The work would be done automatically, right? Wrong!
I was rudely awakened from my state of oblivion, as I sat through an
unexpected assessment so my own understanding of what was going
on, could be determined. Ralph needed to be sure that he and I could
establish some common grounds from which to start the treatment.
He needed to be sure that I was aware of the fact that I'd gone wrong
somewhere along my life's path. He wanted certainty that it was my
own choice to accept this treatment and that I willed, on my own
accord, to beat this disease.

During our first meeting, I was dazed, unfocused and frightened.
I could feel that he was eager to break through a barrier. I had a
mental block still, when accepting more goodness and care. But he
was focused and determined yet gentle and sincere, as he urged me
to provide him with the answers he needed, in order for treatment
to be pursued. I wanted to tell him I knew where I'd gone wrong
and that I was aware of what had become of my life. I wanted to
say the words he needed to hear so as some mental ease would be
felt on my behalf. But I couldn't, because I didn't know anything.
The barriers were still so strong. Ralph's sincere approach meant
breaking point was reached with my cries for help that came
from a deeper source. The tears started flowing from my eyes and
the shameful words started spilling from my mouth, stating that
I didn't know anything about anything anymore!

This particular appointment was the most painful part of the
treatment, because I had to talk about myself, without having any
recollection of who I was, at that moment in time. It was harsh for
me to almost stand outside of myself and witness the floods of tears
I cried as I spoke the words, 'I just don't know!' However, if I hadn't
broken down in such a way, it wouldn't have been possible to create
any kind of connection with him. Only with a certain connection,
could the healer and the patient, or the wizard and I, do the work we
both needed to do.

The depth that the needles reached in the physical body was only superficial, in comparison to the depth that was reached, throughout the whole process of this acupuncture treatment. The needles sat on the surface of the skin, yet the work they actually did, along with the devoted, personal and individual application of the wizard's knowledge, was something that blew me away.

So yes, I was relieved that we reached a base and a foundation from which we were able to work on my health. I knew I needed as much support and guidance from outside of the home environment, so the close and personal relations with my family were affected as little as possible, due to my illness. Ralph was offering me his hand, and I was eager to take it—little did I know where that guidance would lead me. And I was only to find out that destination by attending weekly treatment for as long as I needed. Time was soon to prove that acupuncture would affect my recovery in a profound manner.

On a day like today

On a day like today
I'm tired but strong
My body is weak
But willpower does belong

It belongs to me
It belongs to Fay
Inner strength is there
I can feel it today

It makes me so happy
On days like these
I remember who I am
For Anna is on freeze

This feeling gives me hope
So I have to take what I can
For me to stay aware
That I should ALWAYS give a damn.

Weakness on the outside
But the strength that comes from within
More powerful than anything
Aiming for Fay to win

***

Food is what may seem to have been the issue but it wasn't the root of the disorder. It was the 'ingredient', the 'channel', the 'passage', the 'substance', the 'key' or the 'method' I'd been using to promote destruction. It was the source that led me to break down and it was also the source that would lead me to build myself back up again. By reaching an all-time physical low of 31kgs, I was pushing to rebuild a new relationship with this substance as well as with my self.

Seeing as though I wasn't being admitted to hospital, I wasn't going to be force-fed; this is a procedure many sufferers endure. And because hospital treatment simply wasn't on hand—for which, on hindsight, I'm ever so grateful—it was up to Diann, my Mam and myself to start the gradual increase of my daily food intake. This was approached in a most gentle manner, by Diann. She refrained from overwhelming me with a sudden 3000 calories diet, which is the 'normal' procedure. At the start of recovery I was probably eating 400 calories a day. From our first meeting onwards, every week Diann would add a particular food item to my daily intake. It was initially the foods I classed as being 'safe' (meaning those I'd become obsessed with as I believed they were harmless and could be eaten without fear). But my weight was still dropping, even with this gradual increase. So, a few weeks into our therapy sessions, Diann suggested for me to start taking high calorie energy drinks as a supplement. I agreed. To suddenly permit myself to taking three high calorie drinks a day meant a huge hurdle was being overcome. Suddenly 900 calories EXTRA! I did it though!

These drinks weren't like a magic potion that instantly put my physical body back together again. Nor were they providing me with muscle strength and bodily bounce to run, jump and skip around the town. Though they were the extra nutrition I desperately needed so the weight would at least stop dropping.

They provided energy that intensified every emotion I was encountering. They cleared my mind somewhat, which brought some alertness and concentration to my hazy days—since being malnourished meant full engagement with the surrounding world was almost impossible for lack of focus. These supplements actually are starting to sound like a magic potion! Which I suppose is true; they were what I needed and they let me save myself, instead of the saviour being the hospital drip. How grateful I am!

So I never actually stopped consuming food throughout the stages of developing and recovering from the disorder—which is another stereotypical label that society places on those with anorexia. People can assume they NEVER eat! But it's never as straight forward as that. As I'd always been putting tiny portions and ill-varied food items begrudgingly in my mouth.

Mealtimes started bringing every emotion to the surface—emotions associated with heartache. I often cried for the fear of putting on weight, for the pain I felt my stomach, for the frustration of not letting myself have the food, for the harm I was causing myself by eating, for the goodness it represented. I cried for going against my principles and I cried for being trapped. I cried for the guilt I felt for eating, for the shameful need for food and for the control I'd chosen to loose. These were all tears for Anna. I was slowly becoming aware of what her needs and desires were in my life. With every meal I was eating, I was going against her wishes. I pushed for the needs of Fay and hated myself every step of the way.

1 little boost of energy

The supplements give me all this nutrition
It's doing me more good than bad

Treating my body the way it deserves
So then why are they making me feel so sad

They aren't abusing my body
Not to the extremes that I have done

They are making me a healthy person
So then why am I scared of what is to come

This one little boost of energy
Is more than I deserve to gain
I can prove that I can live on air
But hang on, isn't that why I'm now in pain

They say the body needs it
Otherwise a person cannot exist
I'm intelligent enough to know this
But disciplined too much so I resist

Training myself in such a way
That it can live on next to nothing
Months of hard work and obedience
Is now taking its toll on my entire body

Learning to eat again

How did I let it get this far?

What have I done to myself?

Will the answer leave a permanent scar?

***

As I slowly grasped that I was dealing with two forces, I was getting deeper and deeper into the truth of what was behind the illness. I was learning to distinguish the difference between Anna and Fay. This could only become clear with the realization that there was so much more to life than the bodily appearance. I had to learn that this 'so much more' to life, was in actuality FAY. However, when a compulsive cloud overshadows the deeper meaning to life—deeper that what we see in the reflection—then it's a slow process for the clouds to dissipate and for that meaning to be seen.

I tried to step away from the notion that Anna was I and was led to almost suffer an identity crisis. A term never before have I used and have often joked about. But this is truly what I was experiencing. I didn't know who I was, once I'd been told the truth by Diann, 'You are not the behaviour you've been applying. The behaviour is the illness and you are so much more!' That sounded like a foreign language to me. I couldn't grasp or acknowledge what she meant. For somebody so wise and intelligent to tell me I'm something other than 31kgs, a bag of bones and an ugly projection of perfection, was something unheard of! It was like telling an orange they're a pink square! Comprehension of the fact that there was a split personality, took many weeks.

The understanding came during therapy. Week after week, the person I believed in so strongly, sat in front of me, stating, 'Niamh, the orange you thought was orange and round, is actually pink and square.' So who was I to say this wasn't the new truth that would last for an infinity and go so far beyond, once it was found and embraced? I was nothing after all and had to become something! So I would fight to believe that the orange was indeed square and pink! I would change every belief I had and convince myself that I was something other than what the world witnessing as being an ill soul. Turning something into something other than it feels it's meant to be, isn't a done deal. But I knew I could do it. I was familiarizing myself with both Anna and Fay. Anna had already become way too familiar and with familiarity there's safety. However, I felt no more comfort, so I had to start finding Fay. The battle could only commence once I'd witnessed the other competitor, because a battle isn't a battle when there's only one presence!

Letting go of the log ...

Life is a river gushing by
Where I had discovered the log
The log called Anna

I was holding on so tight
She was so safe
She made me feel strong and good
I trusted her judgement
I trusted her with my life

Loved ones
were on the bank of the river
offering me their hand

I doubted my ability and willpower
to do what I knew was right

I didn't think I could make it
I didn't think I would survive

Such a massive challenge

leaving a log so safe
to struggle
to fight

Several attempts are being made
The log must be left behind
Support is cheering me on
Willing for me to finally let her go

I'm trying my hardest
Every minute of everyday
With everything I've got

But the log will always be there
Can I forever resist and say no?

She has been let go
That is one thing I know for sure

For now I'm reaching
I'm battling in the river and its grime

I'm now in between
in the midst of believing
in Anna and in Fay

I will win it eventually
but WHEN
and for HOW LONG…

It's only a question of time

***

What I'd always believed, wholeheartedly, throughout my whole
life was that I was the happiest person on the planet, without
ever taking into account if those were the actual feelings I was
feeling. I'd been projecting myself as the strong, the invincible, the
independent and the courageous one. I'd lived to be the traveller,
the energy, the health and the achiever. All of these aspects I'd
been attaining due to the behaviour Anna forced on me. So without
Anna, was I still strong, invincible, independent, courageous,
energetic and healthy? Was I the traveller and the achiever?
I didn't feel I was. This is what caused me to crash, and
almost burn.

Who was I, if Anna was somebody else? Who was I, if this
illness wasn't me? I only knew of living and behaving according to
restrictions, punishment and neglect. I only knew of the importance
in standing strong in life and being accomplished in every field
of expertise. I knew of nothing deeper. I'd heard of the 'soul' but
I thought it was basically the beating heart. I thought this beating
heart was only to be felt, sensed and experienced by loving another
person and by being loved by another person. I didn't know that a
person was allowed to love themselves unconditionally. I felt this
to be cheeky and selfish. I felt I didn't have the right to love myself,
especially if I wasn't proving myself or achieving anything. And in
the darkness, I didn't know what was happening but I surely wasn't
reaching any goals!

I questioned so much, as I acknowledged the fact that I was
lost and unaware. I was already fully engaging in the lessons
I could teach myself. My eagerness to learn and my tendency to
overanalyze every encounter in life would never leave my side.
I was so determined to dig wherever I needed to dig so as to find
solutions to everything. I was forcing and trying to speed things
along. I had to get the job done! I had to beat this and I wasn't
going to fail! I pushed, I forced, I analyzed and I wrote. I figured

the more I pushed, the more I would get done and the sooner I'd be cured and on my travels! But this questioning wasn't helping the process of acceptance; with acceptance there comes an ease with the certainty that—in whatever way it's destined to be—things will always work out! I had no ease whatsoever! I had everything BUT ease. I had a disease! I wasn't helping matters, as I pressed against the breakdown, just for fear of giving in to the emotions that were uncontrollable and the mood swings I'd never before experienced in my whole life. The anger would soar through me without warning, the depression would make me cry countless tears and the fear of recovery would petrify me. These were now elements of me! It was my behaviour. My mental self wasn't able to cope with such turmoil that was swirling through my core. This is what felt to be my biggest element of loathe: uncontrollable negativity almost constantly, without my conscious participation.

I felt as though I was letting the illness take ahold of me and that IT was controlling my existence instead of ME controlling the recovery—when really I was very much in control of the pace and the whole process. Still I felt like this outrageous behaviour was who I was. I was convinced I was almost encouraging the moods by not turning them into something positive. In the past, seeing the positive side to everything had always been my strength. Now I was unable and I felt it to be my weakness. I'd been told I wasn't the illness, this I slowly understood. Now, in my inability to see clearly, I'd unknowingly been convincing myself that I was the source of anger, sadness, depression and loneliness. Diann had reassured me that people are not their behaviour; they're a deeper entity of light. It was a slow dawning to convince myself that my outrageous behaviour wasn't the person I had become or was destined to be. So, I wondered where my light was! Was somebody going to give it to me? The fact that I didn't know where it was, was so frustrating and I thought I was never going to find this truth Diann was speaking of. So to say the unease worked with or against my recovery is hard to determine. But it made the darkness approach fast and furious. I like to think that my need for speed was the factor that taught me everything I was destined to learn whilst being surrounded by those shadows—this is just me, looking on the bright side (on hindsight!).

I'm confused.com

The mess that I've created
inside of my head
It's the ongoing war
that forces me back to bed

Stop pushing
Stop pressurizing
Stop forcing
Stop analyzing

Stop in the name of sanity
Stop when it becomes too much

There's only so much a person can take
There can otherwise be too much at stake
Time will tell
Time will reveal all
Time is on my side
Time is all I've got

Don't try to prove it any longer
Don't try to push even when it's stronger
Eventually it will become clear
Eventually I will know what it is

I'm not to let the confusion create a mess
I'm not to let the frustration cause me stress

It all comes with the territory
It's all part of the process

I'm here for a reason
and not because it's easy
I'm not to get freaked out
and just let myself feel queasy

Feeling lost again when days ago I'd been found

My answers of days ago are again transformed into questions

***

To have always believed that satisfaction is experienced only through what I was doing and how I was projecting myself into the world, meant that throughout my life, I'd always been in desperate need of the outside world to provide me with that much-needed seal of approval. It was the eyes of the world I depended on for that feeling of being recognized for how I chose to BE, as a person, within this world.

The force of Anna had once chosen for me to BE ill. And so, during the first months of recovery, this state of being was still how the world perceived me. It was still what I was being recognized for. The outside world was still looking and observing and witnessing what I had achieved. Once before, I'd felt this to be the seal of approval that resembled happiness. I was trying to beat the illness. It was the 'seal' I was trying to strip myself bear of. It was almost an impossible task, with the accompanying observing eyes around me. So I needed to turn away from what others were saying and from what they were seeing (being ME). I didn't want to hear what they were expecting of me nor how they chose to perceive me. Every single word or expectation that I sensed my loving friends and family to give me or to have of me, was something that pushed me to self-destruct a little bit more. Why? Because Anna was still within. She saw the observing eyes and heard the judgemental words and used them as the fuel to harm me and push me to more deterioration.

So, I chose to sit in the darkness. It's where recovery had already brought me and that's where I needed to stay. What a blessing to already have been forced to turn away from the people around me, who were suddenly becoming the reflection of my self. They were showing me what I'd done and who I'd become!

For the longest part of my recovery I couldn't look anybody in the eye, as it caused me such shame. Every interaction, every smile, every gesture, every complement. Everything was all so very wrong and being confronted was the encouragement that forced me to sink deeper into a black hole making it almost impossible for others to communicate with me and express their heartfelt concern. I didn't need any help. In the darkness the only help I accepted from friends and family, was through email. I connected as little as possible through speech.

Bad timing

It was just one sentence coming from the heart
I know she meant so well but it hurt me so bad

Bad timing is all it was but caused me to crumble
A stab to the heart would have been less painful

Feeling so angry towards her followed straight away by guilt
How could I react so badly to someone wanting me to be happy?

Crying again like a baby whilst wanting this turmoil to end
Worn out worrying that people will never ever understand

In turn my plate won't be emptied as I'm tired fighting
The battle between myself and I as I'm praying for it to stop

The focus shifts from what's important to what's not
What and who to care about
how far and in which direction to push

She is standing her ground and I feel it inside
Anna becomes stronger to protect herself from health

Good health is sent by means of 'all is going well'

Ignore them
or the other direction will appeal
and will be followed

***

The course of learning HOW to fight, who I was fighting AGAINST and who I was fighting FOR, was a process that started where the priority lay: food. I was fighting with FOOD against STARVATION for the LOVE OF LIFE. I needed to become conscious of who was controlling me in the moments of eating. I needed a reason to live and a reason to eat. And Fay was that reason, even though I was still only becoming vaguely familiar with her presence. I didn't yet know who she was, so I didn't know why I was eating or how to contact her. Every bite of food I consumed needed to be in aid of fighting Anna—that's all I knew at this stage. Her nutrition was my restrictive behaviour and my starvation. As the saying goes, 'you can't fight fire with fire', so I needed water to fight her flames. I couldn't use starvation as my weapon to fight. Her weapon of destruction was a full stomach!

I was pushing myself to access food on my own accord, as it gave life to whatever energy I was permitting myself to BE in that moment. I desperately needed to refuel and to stock up. The mental barriers were still coming down. I was pushing through them. Firstly, by eating mainly my safe foods and secondly, by eating something new each week. The menu was still being increased by approximately 150 calories each week.

In the moments when I was eating, I hated the world. I was doing something I despised, so of course I was a mess! I realized why I was feeling such disgust towards everyone and everything. What I wasn't able to figure out, was why my moods were so out-of-whack, at every given moment—even those moments when I wasn't eating. I was told by Diann many times that the mental clarity and the energy I was receiving from the food, was being used so I would keep feeding myself. My energy was for mental strength and my body needed every calorie so I would keep the re-feeding process ongoing. Anything else that was happening around me, I was almost incapable of dealing with, because of my unstable mind. This instability is what wrecked my head and it was the reason for my moods to be so unpredictable. My moods were constantly foul and volatile. This literally blew my mind. I had no rationality and no relief from the pain. The pressure in my mind never eased because I was trying to break down a wall. There was the fear of food that was stopping me from having a peaceful mind. I was always terrified of what I'd eaten hours, days and weeks ago as well as being petrified for what I'd need to eat over the coming hours, days, weeks, months and years even (in my darkest moments). The anxiety grew for the weight I'd pile on at high speed and for the self-harm I FELT I was inflicting on my body, due to the consumption.

These fears were literally burdening my soul, burdening Fay. They buried her deeply, making it harder for me to have access to her. Worries weighed heavy on my heart and made the anticipation of mealtimes affect my every hour. The actual eating was literally bringing emotions to the surface that I couldn't control throughout the first few months. Moments of clarity were used to convince myself of the necessity of eating. Clarity was used to clear the passage that would allow some connection to develop between both the physical and non-physical sources of life: a connection between food and Fay.

The panic in regards to past sin, future punishment present torture, was becoming stronger because I was eating. The panic was rising because I was no longer weight-watching, calorie-counting or competitively walking. Usually checking the scales, checking calories and exercising would offer me relief. I wasn't doing any of these things anymore, so the relief never came. Panic was simply IN my mental self. This wasn't the only thing I was faced with. The panic caused my emotional self to break down and the physical body was feeling the strain of keeping this inner turmoil somewhat contained so the whole self could still be within this world. To feel the mental and physical strain of the food was an unbearable weight. How could I carry this weight, when I was so weak and lifeless? My body and soul (the physical and emotional embodiment) wanted to unite. My body was crying for food and my soul was crying for food. My soul wanted to live and needed a body in which to do so! It was the mental body that was the wall in between the two. And with every meal, this wall was being broken down. Ever so slowly. Envision the wall of China and a chisel: the wall was my mental barrier and chisel was my every meal. The one doing the hard work: Fay!

I realized I was reversing the symptoms of starvation. In my hardest moments, throughout the first six to eight weeks, I was applying the methods I'd once used in order to strengthen my will to starve. The same application was now my weakest strength to eat. It was the only thing I could think of that would give me access to Fay, during those vital mealtime moments. With every bite, I would question why I was eating this food. What's my reason for eating? What's my reason for living? I would literally try to find an answer that would give me the go-ahead to take lengthy, cautious and aware motions as I was spooning the food from the plate into my mouth. I'd envision the answer and it was a picture of me travelling, backpacking and adventuring. I'd recall my past experiences and the people I'd met, who were so far on the other side of the world—a place I also needed to be. The mantras were no longer to strengthen my desire to starve, but they were now to strengthen my desire to live. No longer were they 'a moment on the lips is a lifetime on the hips' or 'you are what you eat'. I desperately tried for them to be 'we eat today, to experience tomorrow.' Sometimes, most times, when I was using this mantra, a voice could say, 'You don't want to experience the tomorrows, so there's no need to put yourself through so much pain.' The visions I was desperately trying to give power to— those visions of travels—were deeper and more meaningful.

I would have dreams and nightmares of food. It was all I could think of, fantasize about and see. I prepared my own meals and I ate according to the daily menu that was still gradually expanding each week—just like I felt to be. I looked on in both disgust and admiration as to how easily and happily my family would eat. It was mind-blowing to witness their capability to eat and smile, to eat and talk, to eat and walk, to eat and live. I needed to desperately experience that too! What an amazing life that would be! I wondered if I'd ever felt that same ease when eating, before Anna started to control my life. My memory had been erased and I was now an alien, whilst feeding myself. I knew I had to keep going or else I'd never be like the rest! So I continued pushing through feeling physically sick for constantly needing to eat. I switched off to my cravings for hunger, I forced the meals, I pushed through the thoughts and I ploughed for the answers in a desperate attempt to make sense of the illness, hoping to offer myself some relief.

Sick to my stomach

Trying so hard
to ignore the way I feel
So sickly and full
it feels so wrong

How could I do this
make myself feel this way

When will the feeling of hunger come along
Will that feeling ever be mine again
The one I love and therefore try to prolong

It's hunger I want, need and thrive upon
But for days now
it seems to have gone

I long for it
so badly
I cannot describe

The emptiness and pain
to me it should belong
Has it gone forever
Should I have said goodbye
Is there anything else I can do
to make me feel strong

I'm trying to ignore it and wish it away
A full feeling in my stomach
It's been so long

I could vomit at the thought
and of the amount

It just seems so unnatural
It just seems so wrong

***

What would have offered me relief? No longer being forced by LIFE to eat! Yes! But I knew that was no longer possible. What other options were there? There was no relief in the form of clarity as to what the road to health would present me with. Nothing would ease the way and nothing would ever let me feel happy for eating, happy for gaining weight or happy for choosing health.

I wasn't able to escape from my body and I loathed every ounce of the overweight 32-kilogrammed person I saw looking back at me. Seeing my reflection filled me with such hatred, that it would have only urged me to regain my health—if health meant a better appearance. But at the same time it would only have urged me to continue striving for the perfect reflection, through applying the destructive habits that once had made me feel 'beautiful'. I was being confronted with the 'lies' my honest family and friends were speaking, stating I was too thin. I was confronted with the 'truth' my lying mind was speaking, as it stated I was fat. I couldn't engage with my own mind, because there was nothing I could do anymore in order to loose the weight which I felt was too much. To avoid confrontation, contradiction and confusion, I simply turned away. I knew I had to block the reflection once I realized the mirror was too confusing.

Rejecting my reflection was also done out of pure disgust. Because it was supposed to be my true happiness, but it was a projection of the lies I'd been convincing myself of. It was portraying my truth, my life, my world—it was portraying an illness. Once upon a time my appearance had been the only thing that would offer me my self-worth. And it still very much felt to be that way. I hated it. So how could I ever feel worthy and how could I know who I was, if I judged myself through my mind's lying eyes? My mind was telling me I was orange, when really, I was … pink …?!

So a shift in awareness was being experienced, as I questioned more and more if my judgement was right or wrong. I accused myself of being shallow for having the desire to nearly starve to death, all in aid of being thin. I called myself superficial as I thought I'd intentionally set out to become skin and bone. I couldn't understand why such an illness was being endured, if I wasn't shallow! I had never given such importance to my appearance. I never wanted to loose my life, just to be beautiful! Surely I couldn't be that vain a person! On the contrary! I was simply… me…??!!

I started to judge myself in the same way the vast majority of society would judge those with an eating disorder, because I knew no better. I needed answers. The questioning was the learning process I had to go through. My identity wasn't the illness, nor was it my behaviour—so now I believed my identity was a shallow, vain and superficial person! I was simply digging and digging to come up with answers I thought were right so I could let go of what it was it was I clinging to. I didn't know right from wrong anymore. I was a bad judge and the worst critic because all my answers were wrong! For some reason though, I was succeeding— in my failure—and achieving—in my incompetence.

Reflection of both inside & outside

The way I look is bad
The way I feel is bad
Are they balanced
Are they equals

Do I feel as bad as I look
Do I look as bad as I feel

Does my outside
make me feel worse on the inside?
Does my inside
make me look worse on the outside?

Does one strengthen the other?
Does one wear the other down?

Feeling better will make me look better
Looking better will make me feel better

That explains why I cannot bear the sight of myself
That explains why I feel rotten and old
It should clarify what I'm dealing with
It should clarify why I'm down in the dumps

Some days I will have a look
Other days I refuse

Seeing what I want to see
Believing that what I see isn't me

Fooling myself I'm on top of the world
Fooling myself I look fit and healthy

Needing to realize that I am that person
Needing to realize that I am that reflection
It IS Niamh.

***

In my despair, life on the home front was proving to give me the perfect environment so I could deal with all that had become my life. My support system was fitting as it should. How so? It was due to the adaptability practised by my siblings. In the homely surroundings it's inevitable for the moods and emotions to mix themselves. More often than not, the overriding vibe within the home is determined by the person bearing the most weight. In the literal sense, this may not have been me. But figuratively, it most certainly was! So empowering was my depression and I can only imagine how hard it was for my siblings to watch somebody they love to suddenly become someone unrecognizable. My Mam was up close and personal, due to her attending my weekly sessions. She never missed a beat. However, for my youngest sister Eileen and my brother Sean, it was different. I closed myself off from them and didn't give them an ounce of my attention, energy or focus. I shared nothing with them and rejected their presence as much as I could. Yet they never rejected mine. My rejection of course would have affected them in some manner. Depression may sit within the soul of one person, but anybody in close proximity can't help but be influenced.

To this day, when I think back to how understanding they were, I'm blown away. Their natural ability, in their young ages (back then, Sean was fourteen and Eileen was twenty), to give me exactly what I needed throughout the hardest months, was something that will stand in their favour, throughout the rest of their own lives, as well as mine. For them to never have put any pressure on me, or hound me to open up, to smile, to laugh or to eat, left me at peace with my own inner commotion. They didn't expect me to be cured at the drop of a hat. Instead they accepted me for all that I was. They didn't search for explanations and by doing so, they let me experience my darkness in a lighter shade than it otherwise could have been experienced. They grew through the process with me and, together with my Mam, they formed a homely environment that provided unconditional love. How grateful I am and will always be. Not only my two youngest siblings, but also my older sisters Emma and Orla will always be considered the greatest. I realized that they felt helpless at times, due to them living in Holland. This could have been the blessing in disguise. It meant I felt less pressure whilst still having access to all the support in the world, whenever I'd send out a cry for help through my blog.

I'm inclined to say it's strange, how close people become when an illness is within the family. But instead, I'm going to say it's a gift. An illness can bring out sides of people that were once unrecognized, when they choose to offer support. It can strengthen the already existing relationships. One person in particular, my cousin Mark, felt to have come falling out of the sky, as if out of nowhere. He was suddenly there, with emails and texts. I felt he was living and breathing the illness with me, throughout the first months. Again, strange is what I'm inclined to call it, however a gift is what I'll instead refer to. I know of the extreme measures he went to, so as to educate himself on the illness. This meant he was able to relate to what was going on in my own head and pull me through, aiming for me to keep on fighting. It was really amazing. Many times, throughout this period, I wondered why he—as well as many others—would waste their time wanting to help someone like me. I grew to learn that it's called … unconditional love. How precious.

Forever in debt

Support:
It comes from everywhere
Different shapes
Forms
Sizes

Forever
I'll be so grateful
Words cannot ever describe

The feeling it gives someone just to know
That there is always someone there
Just right THERE
But not knowing where THERE exactly is

We come to depend on people
We would have never thought possible
Never dared dreaming
What would have become without them

Saying 'thank you' is never enough
When something so huge is at stake
Two little words in return for health
Two little words in return for a life

I say it too much to people I love
It seems to become meaningless

When repeated so often
Words become shamefully empty

By never forgetting the extremes
By always cherishing my nearest
By feeling their joy as well as pain
And by remaining
forever
joyfully
in debt

***

 **3**

SEPTEMBER 2008

A new stage approached and I was trying to change my interpretations. What I once had considered to be 'right', was suddenly supposed to be 'wrong'. What I once considered to be 'wrong', was suddenly supposed to be 'right'. I was desperately learning to live according to the new belief that Anna was wrong for my life and that Fay was right for my life. And by trying to change, I was constantly asking myself the same question, 'Who's controlling me?'

The unpredictability of my moods was still very much ongoing as I started to feel the difference in the two energies. From one day to the next, I never knew what to expect. I never knew how I would be, what I would feel and how I would cope with simply living. I started to witness these outbursts of tears, sadness, pain, anger and frustration. I couldn't yet control them however I acknowledged slowly they were the destructive power of the disorder. So I had to let them be. I was starting to have moments where it all made such sense—mainly moments when I was at ease. Sense emerged slowly but surely and the dawning clarity didn't make the regular breakdowns any easier, nor did it offer relief. Clarity actually intensified my feelings of being trapped inside a body that was weak due to the control of the constant unsatisfied and volatile mind. Sometimes I'd realize—as the episodes were happening— who it was that was controlling my empowered outbursts of misery. Other times, it took deep reflection to become aware of what power I was giving life to. I'd process every single detail and learn by writing and speaking of my chaos with Diann.

I never stopped eating, no matter how much Anna controlled me. And so, it became her mission to still dominate me, in as many other areas of my life as possible. She continued to tell me I was a sinner with every waking and sleeping hour—since I had food passing through my body. For Anna it never mattered what time of the day or night it was, the demon would come out and my thoughts would convince me of every lie that had ever been told, just to stop me from doing anything that would be good for me. I wasn't allowed to smile, to laugh, to talk, to hug or to enjoy. I was allowed to do nothing because I was eating. She took over my mind filling me with fears of the road ahead—the road that would inevitably lead me to gain weight, to become obese and to struggle for the rest of my life. She wouldn't let me speak, connect or engage with others. She wouldn't let me take on complements and she wouldn't let me look anybody in the eye. She wouldn't let me get close to my family—even if it was for a hug. My thoughts were telling me I wasn't deserving of any goodness, nourishment, attention or comfort. In my mind I was the deceiver, the non-achiever, the scum of the earth. I was doing something she didn't want me to do, regardless of how low I was feeling. I couldn't fight against any of these fears, for lack of strength. She always seemed to be sitting on my shoulder—observing.

Worlds apart

Feeling so miserable
words cannot describe
Having so much anger
just wanting to express
Wanting so badly
not to feel this way
Is this just a mood
that I'll soon detest

It goes on and on
like it's never going to end
When feeling so down
feeling good seems so far
It could be impossible
to get that feeling back
That feeling of reaching
for your lucky star

Why is the difference
so unbelievably big
Between feeling so good
and feeling so bad

What was the reason
for inventing such doom
Can someone benefit
from feeling so sad

It's a head wrecker the moods
being up and down
Exhausting because
they are worlds from each other

But on a time scale so close
almost face to face
Each mood always trying to fight
being smothered

How can the human body
be capable of such things
It's scary the thought that
we aren't able to control
Such a powerful force
everything is uncertain
What else can we do
other than act out the appointed role?

***

The road felt to be getting harder, even though I was leaving the darkest stage. This was for the fact that my appetite was changing. I was becoming accustomed to switching off to Anna. For weeks I'd been eating and eating, without ever having any sense of hunger. I simply forced it, without taking into account the signals between the stomach and the brain or the body and the mind. After two months, my digestive system was starting to absorb more food as my metabolism was speeding up. And the sudden and unfamiliar hunger pains caused my head to freak out. I used to say 'yes' to hunger and 'no' to food, all at once, and this was my strength, my right! So I still felt that to say 'yes' to hunger and 'yes' to food, all at once, was wrong.

By feeding myself through the darkness, I'd landed myself in a place where my body was becoming aware of food, whether it made me happy or not. I had to deal with it. However, even though clarity was slowly arising, one thing would remain very blurred. I had no remembrance of what foods my body had needed in the past or what portion sizes I used to eat! It was like my memory had erased everything that had been related to food up until Anna entered my life. I wanted to cling to how I used to eat before she ever hit me, but I couldn't remember. I felt it would be safer to relive the patterns of my past food intake, by applying them in my new eating regime. But this was impossible. My new eating patterns were based on my current nutritional needs.

By leaving hunger-mode I was forming a new base so as to rebuild the relationship I'd destroyed between myself and food. My stomach and my brain were learning to send each other the correct signals. I was starting to feel more hunger. So whenever this occurred my stomach would signal to my brain to eat—a normal course of events! I had to ignore Anna, when the hunger was felt—for me, an abnormal course of events.

At mealtimes my stomach would be full after only a few bites, but I needed to have the whole serving so that my nutritional needs would be met. Any other reason, such a pleasure in emptying the plate, didn't come into the picture—eating was a sin! But I would keep on eating. My brain was never easily satisfied—not now that the barriers had come down between myself and particular foods from which I'd deprived myself. As well, my mind knew there was still the possibility for starvation to, once again, be endured. With the constant food increase and the endless mealtimes, my stomach was saying, 'No more food!' My mind was saying, 'More, more, more!' Needless to say there was an imbalance and I was retraining my stomach and my brain, or my body and mind, to become in-sync once again. Everything was changing and my mind didn't know if my stomach was telling the truth nor did my stomach know if my mind was telling the truth. Neither one knew what the others plans were!

This is where the binge-eating started to become a fear. I'd faced these episodes in the past, throughout the development of the illness. I was now reversing the cycle and literally pressing rewind in an attempt to undo the damage I'd done. I was always terrified of never being able to stop eating, once I started. The dangers of binging and losing control, was something I desperately needed to be in charge of, otherwise the guilt that Anna would place on me after the act of binging, would be unbearable. The guilt already had become an overriding and an inevitable element of this re-feeding process. It was Anna's way of keeping her claws into me. I was a sinner after all! And when a crime is committed, guilt arises! Her guilt, which was my guilt, would lead me to battle against my desperate urgency to punish myself for the sinful act of eating (punishment in the form of eating less). Therefore the main reason to avoid binges was to avoid later restriction. I needed to keep feeding myself in a controlled manner, no matter what!

Playing the game

A feeling that cannot be described
You cannot express it with words
It's empty and hollow
As well as full and stuffed
Wanting more knowing you should
But not wanting to give in
Self-loathing then follows the debate
Because you want it
But you're not allowing yourself
But others want you to
And your body tells you it needs it
But there's still something else
Something inside that says no
It says it's against the rules
The rules you have lived by
The rules that would make you a better person
If you go against them you'll be a bad person
Then you're being disobedient
Like a little girl you should then be punished
That's also not allowed anymore
All the rules you would abide by
They have become empty
They have become meaningless
So what rules are you supposed to live by now
Who is going to tell you the new ones
How will you know if they are the right ones
It's unfair to change the rules, so far into the game
Doesn't that mean it's game-over
Do you have to start all over again now
Have you started obeying the new rules already?

Eating that muesli bar last night at 8.30
Was that a new rule you must follow
You don't think you like this new game that much
It doesn't make you happy or feel good
The players in this new game
They are nicer than the other players
But still this game is so much harder
It's got so many more levels
You were nearly finished the other game
You were nearly near the end
You were nearly a winner
But now
You're not too sure
Will you have enough lives
Will you get to the highest level
They say practise makes perfect
But you have to learn the new rules first
Or else you can't play the game
When you can't play
It will constantly be game-over
Then you'll get frustrated
Because you're not getting anywhere
That's when it's crucial
That's when you'll want to give up
You won't want to play the game anymore
Not until you know you're getting better at it
Loosing all your lives means game-over
Getting to the highest level means game-over
You wonder if you've been building up your score
You wonder if this score will give you extra lives
How many attempts
How much patience

How many lives
Keeping the rules simple
And your head clear
Concentration
Focus
Determination
Keep on playing…
See how far you get...

***

The guilt I felt for eating was something I couldn't comprehend. All I knew was that I felt it because I was doing something wrong by Anna. By choosing to recover, I was choosing to sit with this feeling. This urged the shady truths to the surface. And what were they? What was I being faced with by sitting with guilt and continuing to eat according to my daily menu?

I'd been told by Diann that shame is the underlying issue. Feeling guilty urges us to behave differently. That way we can wipe away the shame. In terms of eating and feeling guilty: to act on my guilt would've stopped from eating. Restriction would then commence. This would have caused the shame to sink once again. Guilt can only be dealt with, when a person sits with it long enough. It then gets to a stage where it becomes overbearing and a person can do nothing else, other than find out where the shame originated. This is what I did. I had to force myself to 'sit it out' and I didn't give guilt the power to control my actions. By doing so, the truthful origins for my feeling of shame, started to appear. The root became more and more evident, the more I permitted myself to eat, the more I permitted myself to live, the more I permitted myself to simple be … me. Suddenly I found I was ashamed to be … me. I was starting to touch the source!

Eating my way to the bottom of my soul is what I was starting to experience. Looking back, it was like I was eating myself away from the old belief system I'd set up within and eating myself towards the new belief system, in an attempt to gain my freedom. But this acknowledgment didn't empty me of the guilt that was seeping through my whole core, with every bite I ate. It only let me become slowly more distant from the urges I had to actively engage in the guilt—which would have been done by stepping away from food. However the guilt and the underlying shame still ruled my days for many months. I knew that my shame was also linked to the fact that I was failing to still put my faith and belief in Anna. She was still overpowering, hence my feeling of being a failure in her eyes. After all, I was eating, I was living, I was being. I was simply failing at feeding Anna her hunger. I was feeding Fay her life and filling my soul with guilt. But I would continue to eat through the process of change I was experiencing.

It was only by living through both guilt and fear that I would eventually be controlled by Fay—that deeper source of support and guidance that would help in dealing with Anna's control.

A feeling of ...

A feeling of hunger
Third day in a row
A feeling of guilt
Its rising isn't slow
A feeling of control
It's starting to fade
A feeling of fear
For me it's made
A feeling of loss
The voice will soften
A feeling of stress
So much and so often
A feeling of weakness
With each and every bite
A feeling of disgust
But still winning this fight
A feeling of victory
Doesn't feel as it should
A feeling of hate
And still tall is how I stood
A feeling of disbelief
That it's a battle I'll win
A feeling of sadness
Because I'll never be thin
A feeling of rage
That this will never end
A feeling of strength
As I remind myself
my life isn't pretend

***

The weekly acupuncture treatment started off slowly. The treatment itself would always follow a talk and evaluation of the week gone by. Ralph needed to know how much I was eating and how I was physically feeling. I always struggled to spill my thoughts. I had so much anger when speaking of food. So I was wary of letting him too close, for fear of being misunderstood. I needed to not shy away. I had to resist being pushed away by Anna when Ralph would ask questions and give suggestions in regards to my food intake and my general well-being. I felt mentally challenged throughout these talks. I was so withdrawn, yet so eager to take his help. I felt I could only participate so much. I pushed myself however, each week, so as to give him some leeway. He needed to know at least what my physical self was going through. Even if it was a huge challenge to speak openly to anybody other than Diann, about such things—especially if my words were confirming that I was working hard to beat Anna. This made me feel to be such a shameful failure.

Having said that, during these moments of trying to connect, I knew and felt how sincere and understanding he was. It takes a certain individual, who isn't trained to treat sufferers of any eating disorder, to deal with the bleakness the sufferer carries with them throughout the early stages of recovery. It takes somebody who has a deeper understanding of the mental barrier that sits, not only between the sufferer and food, but also between the sufferer, the world and all the people within it. The fact that he had an open mind and an open heart, compensated for my own closed mind and empty heart. It made the treatment possible.

The world of acupuncture opened up a world inside of me. I learned through taking to the treatment, just how much our bodies rely on energy and balance in order to function properly. I realized that my own body was out of balance; physically, emotionally and mentally. I became aware of the how fragile the individual is and how much it depends on the owner, to look after it (how simple and naive that may sound!). I never knew, for instance, that our health depends on energy to move in a smooth and balanced way through a series of channels beneath the skin and that these channels connect the interior and the exterior physical body to each other. I had no recognition of the fact that the physical flow of life energy becomes disturbed when an illness arises. I had no recollection of the fact that in order to bring the desired physical balance back to how it should be, the needles injected during acupuncture treatment in the upper layer of the skin, are to stimulate that flow of life. This was all news to me!

Ralph taught me these things. It was what I was open to taking from him and it was his area of expertise. He also enlightened my own physical ailments that I never knew before existed. I was suffering from a weakened spleen (which is responsible for the creation of energy that comes from food, along with holding the internal organs in place). This weakening was caused by malnutrition and would ultimately affect the internal organs, resulting in a lack of energy, no appetite, bloating of the stomach, constipation, no periods and a disrupted digestive system. He assured me that once the treatment would start to work, I'd feel hungry, eat more and my digestive system would be stimulated. This would lead to a bigger appetite and provide me with more nutrition that would, in turn, stimulate the blood supply and ultimately create more energy, strength and balance.

I was still trying very much to come to terms with accepting this extra help, so hearing of such goodness was initially a frightening realization. But in my good moments, it excited me deeply. Because I realized I wanted the balance and energy he was telling me of! It was a new reason for me to eat! Still it scared Anna and she was freaked out to think that somebody was working on my body so it would take in more food and gain weight! But the fact that Ralph was determined and strong-minded, made me want to prove to him that I could do this. It made me stronger to desperately achieve better health.

The moments of being on the treatment table (which would last usually forty-five minutes to an hour) were always heavenly. It never mattered if Anna was on my shoulder. The acupuncture was always relieving. Throughout the first weeks the treatment was mainly focused on promoting relaxation and releasing tensions and stresses that needed to be overruled. I did my utmost to savour the moments, no matter how much Anna wished to reject the free and light feelings that would be experienced throughout that blissful hour, each week.

Daydreaming the day away

Daydreaming and escaping to a far away place
Floating upwards into space
Without a barrier or obstacle in sight
The planet is explored on this endless flight

Fearless of the destination
No troubles or frustrations
Reality has been left behind
All by the power of the mind

Daydreaming and escaping the here and now
Drifting away but not knowing how
Any goal you set you will easily achieve
Anything is possible in the world of make believe

Without hesitation or doubt
No matter how events turn out
The opportunities are yours
And it's a world of open doors

Daydreaming the moments we hope that will arrive
Feeling exactly what makes us thrive
We write the script from beginning to end
The daydream is lived and doesn't feel pretend

Needless to say or suggest
The energy felt is at best
It's your creation
Your screen
Your rules, your team
After all it's
YOUR DAYDREAM

***

 **4**

OCTOBER 2008

I once felt the darkness was a place I'd never leave. So powerful it was, especially because it was the first time to ever experience any level of depression. When I was there, I couldn't see anything. Due to the darkness to have been so intense, heavy and blinding, once the change started to happen, I was gradually able to feel it and see it; different shades of grey were holding a stronger presence. My mind was miraculously creating space for light to enter. Light can feel positive and good. This wasn't the case in my situation. The reason for this stage to have felt harder than the stages I'd already passed through, was because I saw that my life was only allowed to continue WITHOUT Anna.

Tearing myself away from something that felt to be a part of me, resembled going through a break-up. I had many moments of literally having an aching heart at the thoughts of no longer living for Anna. I felt to be loosing something special, unique and safe. I felt torn to shreds deep down inside and I cried countless tears throughout this period. It was a rare day if my eyes stayed dry. I'd been heartbroken in the past over a certain guy. This time around, my heartache wasn't over somebody outside of myself, but over somebody inside. The constitution, the genetic makeup and the nature of the so-called person for whom my heart was aching, was different. The pain felt just as intense, and it wasn't until this point in time that I realized just how much a part of me Anna was.

Phrases came to mind that resembled the loss of something that I'd taken for granted. I had statements stuck in my mind, 'you don't know what you've got 'till it's gone' and 'till death us do part'. All the others, such as, 'in sickness and in health' and 'for better or worse', they were all forgotten. Because for Anna the only statements she valued was, 'till death us do part'. There was no 'better' for her, there was no 'health'. Nothing of the kind. When I was feeling heartbroken this statement was a strange comfort, as it dawned on me that living with her meant no life at all. Death would be where we would part, if she'd have had her way. Yet, I still felt less of a person and I felt incomplete. I'd lost my other half.

I started to look at the relationship I'd had with her, as one being destined to fail. It wasn't based on love, because this wasn't what she was giving me. Yes, in the beginning she did. I felt so much 'love' for myself! But just like many bad relationships—where the other half is the dominator, the ruler, the controller—the love is felt in the beginning. Empty promises of happiness are so fulfilling, for as long as the two stick together. The controller tends to first project themselves as being the force and the power that's needed by the other more impressionable and vulnerable of the two. It's the controller on whom the weaker one starts to depend, as proof to the world they are something unique. Lies are told by the dominator that the more sensitive one is indeed incapable of living without their powerful presence. The dominator takes control of the relationship by convincing them they're unworthy in the absence of their power and only standing strong in the world with the controller and dominator by their side. Sticking together leads to a merging of the two and suddenly there's only one. Then, when it comes to the break-up, only does the impressionable and sensitive one realize just how deep the false connection was. They realize it was a relationship based on broken promises alone.

The distance was increasing. I felt this so strongly. And so scared I was, as I faced the road ahead that only seemed full of absence of love for everything. Rebuilding a new relationship with my self is what I needed to do. I needed to start learning to depend on my self and on my own strengths to make it in life. I was told by Diann I was establishing new foundations and I needed to believe in the inner power I was developing that would guide me throughout the rest of my life.

Heartbroken

A breaking heart
aching like hell
It tears me apart
there's nobody to tell

The grief, the sorrow
words could never say
The aching, the pain
all felt by Fay

A breaking heart
for someone so wrong
It tears me apart
because you'll never belong

The loneliness, the fear
nobody else can ever know
The longing, the emptiness
has taken away my glow

A breaking heart
like never before
It tears me apart
for you were who I'd adore

The disbelief, the outrage
of what you put me through
The exhaustion, the nothingness,
I'm now left with,
because of you.

***

To start believing that I could live without her and to start trusting myself, was huge. I figured if I'd once gone so wrong and had made myself so ill, then surely I'd never be able to make a decision again that would be right! I still had no clue of what was right and wrong and therefore a sense of panic would arise at the thought of making my own decisions in life, that were meant to be based on honesty.

I needed to know how I would ever be able to trust myself again now that I'd lost the only thing I'd believed would bring me happiness. Listening to Diann's words, I was assured I was discovering and growing in something that would stand in my favour for the rest of my life. With a heart that feels like it's breaking, it's so hard to properly hear kind words of wisdom from somebody outside of oneself. The feelings can be too intense to ignore. To become distant from the grief—even if it's only for a moment—is sometimes the hardest part. But I did experience moments when I was able to do so. Those were precious moments during therapy, moments when I was writing and moments when I was flying on Ralph's treatment table. In those instances I knew my heartbreak was over something that would never bring me happiness and would never guide me safely throughout my life. So I was able to look at my situation and my health through the healthy eyes of Fay. I'd feel wholeheartedly the honesty in what Diann was saying as she answered to my panic, 'You're in the process of developing something that will guide you always.' When I felt her words, those were moments when Fay was in charge. I was tapping into exactly what she—the guide outside of myself—was referring to: my inner guide, my intuition.

The inner guide can have many different names. Some call it instinct, gut feelings, impulses, insights, feelings or intuition. Others may call it their angels. At first I'd been referring to Fay as basically being the healthy side of myself. But I was slowly referring to her as my guide. She was becoming more and more the extra sense I was tapping into. I was tearing myself away from the powerful mind so I could be guided by something deeper. It was my heart that would only ever offer me the happiness I knew I, for some unknown reason, deserved.

Hearing from Diann that by maturing my intuition I was steering myself away from Anna, meant I was also receiving the answer to the age-old question. The one being, 'Is it better to follow the head or to follow the heart?' I was learning already that by following the heart, I would heal myself. Throughout my whole life I'd wondered which guide was best and which one would guarantee happiness. It was either one or the other. I'd been told it was the head, as the heart would only lead to pain! Passion, magic and dreams lie within the heart. And this is what I never understood whilst growing up: how could something so magical, cause pain? Nobody around me ever gave an answer that coincided with my gut feelings. The answers were now coming to me as I was breaking free. The answers had been stored away in my heart. Now they were revealing how happiness is experienced. I was to follow my intuition, my heart. I was to become someone who based their decisions on personal and unique passions, dreams and desires, regardless of what the world was to say. I knew a new way of life was slowly going to appear. However there were still clouds overhead making it nearly impossible for me to see anything that could have resembled a beautiful clean, clear and crisp skyline. But I was desperate to pursue. I was becoming someone new. Even if those clouds were still thick, heavy and a darker shade of blue.

Not just a doll

She sits by the bed, always guiding
As well as protecting, looking, pushing and minding
Without knowing what she really means
I actually knew all along, or so it seems
Already thinking the right things, before I knew why
Tells me my guide always knew I could fly
Not predicting but sensing everything is positive
Getting me there, has always been her prerogative

She sits, she's quiet, she's humble, she's sweet
I hug her and tell her I'm so happy to meet
A symbol of myself, once so small and frail
Someone who has never judged me, even if I'd fail
She was always there, but not within vision
I never knew that ignoring her would cause a collision
Nourishing her, is letting me see the way
She'll never again leave my side, come what may

She's there, she's proud, and oh so strong
And knows that with me, is where she'll belong
Trusting her knowledge and learning to hear
Because the answer is there, it's louder than the fear
I take her in my arms and embrace her fully
Never to mistreat her, as I'm not a bully
She was given a gift, to force where needs be
My doll, my Fay, my intuition, it's all me…

***

The combination of therapy and writing was creating space in my mind. And when the mind has more space, it will try to clear things up. It will look for solutions, it will pose questions, it will analyze. These were things I'd already been doing, when I was in the darkness. But back then I couldn't see anything. I was digging but unable to rationalize, unable to start piecing the puzzle of my life together. With more clarity I was now eager to arrange my life. A life that HAD to be different. It had to be a life without deprivation, restrictions, punishment, self-loathe and destruction. I had to refrain from slipping back into the behaviour that had led me to endure the illness in the first place.

If a person has been training the mind for years, with the aim of living according to certain principles—so as to deal with life—then patterns resembling pathways have been set up in the mind. It's the conditioning. When trying to re-programme the brain, by practising different ways of living, new pathways can be created. I was slowly trying to carve new ways. I was getting away from the mind that had been tamed by Anna. With the dawning clarity of what I needed to do, I longed to see the world around me through clearer eyes too. But it wasn't clear. There was a constant danger of slipping into old patterns of bad behaviour. The mind is a lazy tool and once it's set up in a particular manner, it doesn't feel the need to change. Whenever it's given the chance to relax, then that's what it will do. Suddenly the old pathways are the guide once again! With so much focus I was forcing my mind to adapt, even if it would have preferred to have simply enjoyed the ride of life— whilst being in control! No! That wasn't my way forward!

Creating something new is unknown, unsafe and unfamiliar. The way in which the mind copes with such unfamiliarity is by filling the whole body with fears—hoping these fears will steer the 'driver' (which needed to be Fay) back to the road that's safe (which was still trying to be Anna). But my urgency to plan, to move, to clarify and to analyze, meant I was digging for answers regarding my past as well as my future. This was causing me to fear absolutely everything. So I instead needed to look into the NOW. I'd been told that's where all the answers would present themselves. I had to realize that I could only find out what would eventually lie ahead, once I'd found out what was lying beneath.

Looking into the now, meant being present in my own situation. My homely surroundings were offering me a place of peace— something I hadn't let myself experience, since I'd always been on the run and partaking in the race of life. This 'present state of being' became more important and it took less effort as time passed by. This was not only due to the body having broken down, but also due to the acupuncture sessions. One hour of treatment a week was enough to relax my body so much so that many valuable moments of ease were being experienced. And in these moments certain things were brought to my consciousness. The biggest revelation I remember to have had, was finding out that 'I' was capable of holding such power, that subconscious destruction is what had been accomplished. I realized the source of death was within my beliefs and it was a harsh reality. I'll never be able to put into words what the exact feelings were, once I realized this simple fact of the matter. I'd been told that anorexia was a mental disease and I knew of the identity crises I was going through. But it wasn't until I, MY SELF, made this actual 'click' that I truly realized I had become so ill by the power of the mind alone; it had been MY power! I was blown away by sheer astonishment of what a human being is capable of.

Power of the mind

Forever thinking you're invincible
Not knowing the truth
Forever thinking you can cope
Not feeling the drowning

Forever the mind is controlling
Being guided by your subconscious
Forever acting according to thoughts
Being unaware of the reason

FORVER suddenly has another meaning
It's your own lifetime
Your FOREVER is made up of thoughts
Living and breathing

These thoughts are somehow created
They have their own identity
These thoughts are buried and stored
They will grow until FOREVER
These thoughts will become you
They are the reason for your decisions

FOREVER appears sooner than expected
The thoughts are identified
Everything clear but also hazy
Things that FOREVER seemed true
no longer exist

A person is lost as well as found
Caused by actions that have led to a certain place
A person shall deal as well as heal
Caused by the mind telling them it's time

The mind has never failed to let you down
Processing the happiness, sadness, torture and pain
The mind has been pushing you through life
Structuring, programming and filing each moment

The moments you have lived and experienced
They are used by the mind in a way to help
The feelings you have hidden or treasured
They will arise to offer the clarity you seek

Every single one is taken on board
You rely on a thought to become an action
Every single action you take
You rely on your mind to know it's right

Therefore never be scared
You're strengthening and healing
And have faith in yourself
Just never fight the feeling

***

I was four months into my recovery and I was taking to food. During the first months, I'd passed through a few stages. Initially I'd been eating in order to avoid hospital admittance (I was forcing food down my throat without taking any feelings into consideration and instead only visualizing the dream I was meant to be living by travelling the world.) Then I landed in a period of eating continuously, always feeling full and occasionally feeling the contradictive hunger, all at the same time. During both stages I'd had stomach pains, bowel problems, a constant feeling of sickness and regular floods of tears for the shameful act of accepting food. Now though, I was slowly eating myself towards a new stage.

Infrequent hunger pains were becoming more regular. My body was digesting food with less discomfort. Physically I was sucking everything I could from the 2500 calories I was eating each day. My weekly menu was nevertheless still being increased and fear foods were also being faced, all in agreement with Diann—she needed to be the one to suggest what food either could or should be added to my menu. It usually was something containing fat, sauces, sugars, oils or anything I used to consider as being a sinful pleasure and had deprived myself of. Adding to my menu was all in aid of facing and overcoming my fears.

My body was taking energy from the food. I was starting to feel it on a subtle physical level and a more obvious mental level. Why was it so apparent to me, that I had more mental energy? Because when the energy would rise to certain level, I'd feel it so intensely and could do nothing other, than eagerly express the control Anna still had over me. In these instances, I loathed the fact that I was eating, feeling hunger. I was again disgusted for gradually gaining weight. But the hunger was rising and my appetite was growing. So I had to eat. Yet, the more I'd eat, the more I'd give Anna strength. I was trying to feel that I was eating for the good of me, for my health, for Fay. At the same time, by doing so, I felt it to be for the bad of me, because the moods were so destructive. I felt I was literally feeding Anna and no longer Fay. And that's when I hated Fay and didn't really want to eat. The battle often got too much and I could do nothing else, other than go with the emotions whenever they'd arise. I was in a state of utter confusion as to who I was feeding, who I was fighting and what was going on. Moments of writing told me exactly where I was. I knew where I stood. I was stuck in the middle! Smack bang, in between two forces.

This meant I was unsure if I was moving either backwards or forwards. But I was seeing how the recovery process was following a cycle of ups and downs all the time. The emotions would always be moving through me, causing me to rise and fall. The flow was following the course it was meant to and it was a sign I definitely wasn't standing still. That in itself made the journey an adventurous one. I was the one ever 'raring to go' and keen to get things done! So if the emotions were something to get me through this uneasy stage, then I was fighting fit! It was plain to see and feel that I was hungry for more of life.

Hungry for life

I'm so hungry for life and craving to win this fight
I don't know how to feed myself: this dream I have in sight

I was never ever wanting to again feel hungry for food
But hunger plus food equals a life in my own good mood

I'm fighting with myself and know I have to feel
I never imagined that reacting to hunger wouldn't appeal

Why does it scare me? I don't want to feel anymore fear
I just want to enjoy my food without Anna in my ear

It's confusing, frustrating and makes me feel weak
Anna can therefore make my days never-ending and bleak

I hate her so much for taking everything away
And for wanting me to always neglect and punish Fay

Depriving myself of food is preventing myself to live
The goodness the soul can take and that food will always give

But for acting on my hunger pains
I'm causing other things to rise
Things that scare me
And things that I despise

I'm so tired and really want to eat without going mad
I don't want to always feel so guilty, so fat and so bad

I'm so hungry for life
my insides are bursting to be set free
But I'm so scared to feel the hunger
so I need to just be ME

***

The hunger was on the up, just like my appetite. This made others around me so happy but not me. It scared the life out of me. The hunger would be so frequent and so severe, to the point where I'd become weak within a half an hour of eating something I'd class as a proper meal. I needed to avoid the physical weakness and so I'd eat and eat and eat and gain strength on that level, for a short period of time. In gaining that element of strength I would temporarily feel mental weakness, because I'd listened to my body crying out for food and I'd obeyed my own needs. Hunger used to be my friend. It now had become my enemy, as it meant I had to take action and eat.

My body was subtly starting to tell me what and when I needed to eat. If I didn't listen or obey in those moments I was giving Anna power. I knew I would still welcome the feeling of hunger as it would give me back the false strength I was slowly loosing, with the months passing by. I would still have happily sat with hunger. It would have been like revisiting a friend, someone I'd not spent time with for so long! I was always tempted to feed Anna her hunger instead of Fay her food. But I knew what was happening, I was witnessing these thoughts and so I acted according to what my body was crying out for.

But what was Fay's food? What was I supposed to eat in my sinful moments of indulgence? It was up to me! Suddenly Diann wasn't the one to tell me what I needed to eat, when the hunger would present itself. I had to cure my own cravings and I had to give in to eating the foods that had always only been for others, but never for me! Suddenly they were for me TOO!? This was like the world was opening up to me. And I was overwhelmed and terrified when stepping into the supermarket or anywhere that would serve food. I'd been granted permission to have whatever I was in the mood for! This was truly lifting the barriers. It COULD have been like letting a child loose in a toy store, after years of not having had a single thing to play with! Instead it was ACTUALLY letting someone with a fear of water dive into the deep end. Nevertheless, I may have had fears but I was able to swim! I trusted Diann when she told me it was time to obey my hunger, obey my body and give it what it needed. All by myself.

My taste buds were being tickled and I was enjoying food. I was listening to the guilt but I wasn't letting it take away my moments of pleasure! Had food suddenly become enjoyable? Did I like it? Were my taste buds happy and was my mind satisfied? Never was it simple to answer either yes or no to such questions! In moments of leaning towards Fay, it was yes, and I secretly savoured those feelings. In moments of leaning towards Anna, it was no, and I secretly savoured those feelings. So clear I stood in my calm confusion and chaotic acceptance!

Acting on the hunger wasn't a simple deed and it had many consequences. One of the tales I was being told by my unsatisfied mind was that I could overeat on all the bad and feared foods, whilst retraining the internal communication. My mind was convincing me that the illness would then vanish, as if by magic! I often believed so strongly that I could undo the damage, by overeating. What a brilliant solution! But I knew this wasn't the outcome. To try and eat away the issues was just another form of emotional eating. I had to stay strong. Otherwise the guilt-factor would have resulted in an urgency to turn away from food. This would then have been followed by anger, frustration and grief. It was that vicious circle again! The only way to break the circle was through control and persistence, no matter how strong Anna's force became.

I was never sure if I was breaking the circle or not. Me, being the 'researcher', I wondered if I was then restricting by not eating as much as I needed (and giving Anna control) or was I healthily controlling so as to bring balance into my diet (because binging is never something that can promote health, no matter what condition a person may be in). I discussed this each week with Diann and I was told to keep going as I was. She assured me the balance would re-establish itself and the moods would eventually subside. As well, I was regularly told to give myself a break! 'The body and mind are only made to undergo so much, Niamh!' Having said that, I was, and often still am, blown away by what it can actually withstand before it's tempted to give in. Either way, the sum of these factors was enough to wreck my head: confusion, hunger, 2 forces, guilt and overeating. They all pointed to one conclusion: I needed new reasons for food!

Different reasons for food

A bite for life
To fight or feel the pain
A mouthful for strength
To keep on going or to just remain
A chunk for others
They are worthy and I am not
A spoonful NOT for me
To keep what's missing an empty spot
A sip for today
To forget the fears awaiting tomorrow
A piece for the soul
To have energy to express the sorrow

A bite for life
To never forget the reasons
A mouthful for strength
To see us change along with the seasons
A chunk for others
To fool me, myself and I
A spoonful NOT for me
To let Anna bully me and make me cry
A sip for today
To be able to feel a little lost
A piece for the soul
To find it
And cherish it
At any necessary cost

***

Could I search for different reasons for food, now that the few extra kilos and the speedy metabolism were both steering me further and further away from the appearance of needing hospital treatment? Food had once NOT been for pleasure, not for nutrition, not for fun, not for life. But now food actually did have to be for life, for nutrition and for … fun, enjoyment, pleasure?

I knew one thing for sure: food was not to be for the fact that I felt to be sitting in either a thin or an overweight frame (I had no clue if I was fat or thin.) I wanted to use food for the goodness it was starting to offer me. This feeling of goodness was something I'd briefly encountered throughout the process of tuning in to my bodily needs. Those moments were making me acknowledge that relating my feelings to the foods I was eating, had nothing to do with how I appeared in the mirror.

Diann also enlightened me on how closely connected food and mood really are. My fleeting moments of inner enjoyment and pleasure were accompanied by positive thoughts. These positive thoughts were kept in place if my weight was stable and if my food intake was stable. On the other hand, my feelings of disgust, anger and frustration were accompanied by negative thoughts. This negativity would only continue if my weight remained unstable or if it was possibly dropping for lack of nutritional needs. The positive thoughts kept my weight gaining and Fay close and the negative thoughts forced my weight to drop and Anna would remain close. Learning of the close relationship between positivity and Fay versus negativity and Anna, I wanted to feel love for food. I already knew that moments of pleasure made me feel worthy of life, so I needed to keep positive and hang on to stable eating patterns. It was those good feelings that were becoming a deeper reason for food, instead of the desire to be thin, beautiful, perfect and different. As easy and complicated as it may sound, that's exactly how straight forward and confusing it was.

Was this positivity a concrete reason for me to stay on top of Anna? It may not have been tangible but it was at least something to fight for and so, focusing on the increase of positivity was a good start! I knew I needed something more; something that was certain, indestructible, dependable, never based on the voices of the world and never containing empty promises, shattered dreams or broken hearts. Nothing of the kind!! I needed a sacred truth to live for. And it was the most important thing in life that I was slowly gaining access to. The sparks of positivity were a sign of this. They were a sign of LIFE itself! I needed more. I needed to obey my literal hunger in order to feed the hunger of my soul! My soul wanted to live fully again! I needed to eat for freedom! Yes! Food was going to give me the wings I'd lost!!!!!!!!!!!!!

I felt to have made a break through as I established that I needed to use the hunger I was feeling—in EVERY sense of the word—as my reason to keep eating! The logic of life! Food was the source of nutrition and energy. It had already given me a second chance! And I was setting off more and more sparks of that life inside of me and they were bursting more and more to get out. This was the energy and life I needed to fuel, by continuing to eat. I was eating for a new reason! I wanted that energy inside of me to finally be set free!! The energy that was this life and it was granted by the food I was eating! Food was for Life!

Laughter and smiles

A roar of laughter, that makes your stomach hurt
Such a glorious feeling, forgetting the dirt
It awakens your senses and switches you on
Relieves the stress and the worries are gone

Laugh until I cry and tears are expressing joy
Just let go and play with humour as it were a toy
Something I never appreciated or saw as being unique
It's now such a treasure, such a gifted streak

Like so many things I'm longing to regain
Smiles will soon fill the spots that are now pain
A chuckle, a laugh, a giggle, a smile
When I can do this without guilt
I'll have gone the extra mile

***

 **5**

NOVEMBER 2008

The determined self was so eager to already be out in the world again even though I didn't know exactly who I was becoming or what I wanted to project. It was too soon for me to have established a stable relationship within my self. I had to sit tight and continue what I was doing: therapy, acupuncture, resting, writing and eating. Practising patience—which was a challenge—meant I was down and very low. I often felt like more of a failure than when I was in my darkest hours. In those black hours, I didn't need to do anything and I didn't feel the urge to present myself to the world as being anything in particular. I was just … ill. In those stages there wasn't any weight gain and my soulful expression (on my blog) was also black. So it was all fine!

Now however, the determination to MOVE and LIVE was something that pushed me to want to show myself to others. So I was continuously putting myself to the test. I was pushing to place myself in society by holding my head high, whilst conflictingly wallowing in shame, due to the kilos that had accumulated. I felt world was suddenly the witness of my shameful appearance. The shame I experienced was because of feeling judged by the surrounding world for the extra 3, 4 or 5kgs I was suddenly carrying (only to be seen on my face, which was where the weight first gained). The pressure that gathered itself in my mind, due to this shame, collided with the new beliefs and principles I was trying to keep in place and it would make me hang my head heavily because I was accomplishing something that never before had been a reason for me to feel proud of myself. I felt alone, misunderstood and physically worse off than before I actually started recovery. I had to constantly rationalize the emotional anger and frustration that was brought on by the observing eyes of the world, in order to deal with it.

Before recovery started, I believed others would love me more for staying a certain weight—just like I would love myself more for staying a certain weight. Now that I was putting on weight, it was painfully frustrating and overbearingly confronting to STILL feel that my lazy mind was too willing to use another person's judgement as a measurement for the love I felt towards myself— just as I once had done. My mind was STILL urged to use the wrong (and old) principles in life to make me feel happy and whole as a person. At this stage I knew so strongly that I didn't want or need to receive recognition from others for something I was doing in life. This was not how I needed to rebuild my new self. I needed to rebuild my self, without praise, judgement, approval, complements or criticism from anybody in my surroundings.

When I'd put myself to the test by interacting with the people around me and the town in which I lived, I had to mentally stay distanced from the judgement, criticism, stress and pressure that accompanies daily life. I was in the process of stepping away from being controlled by the mind and the ego. I was learning that I was feeling good when my heart was in control and feeling bad when my head was in control. My heart was only in control when I was distant. I wasn't yet strong enough to be controlled by my heart whilst being in out in the world (or stepping outside my front door). I was becoming aware, in general, that the mind is dependent on the control brought on by the surrounding world. It's the one thing that causes pressures to fill our individual worlds. It weighs heavy on the heart—it was weighing heavy on mine. I was learning to only engage in my own feelings and by doing so, I was learning to feel worthy, good and accomplished without anybody in my presence or without doing anything in particular. I was aiming to feel accomplished in nobody's eyes, only mine.

Pride without Achievement

Depending on your values in life
depending on your choices
Be who you want to be
whilst ignoring all the voices

Influences
from the outside-in or inside-out
Take away what you need
or let them go when in doubt

Being proud of who you are
no matter what you decide to do
This doesn't come easy
especially when feeling lonely
sad and blue

Through living your life
and doing what you feel is best
You need not compete
or compare yourself to all the rest

Pointless and insignificant
are words that come to mind
You are just one in a million
yet forever one of a kind

One soul amongst the billions
with whom you share this earth
Only to realize
there was already a world with lives,
before your birth

Feeling such importance
whilst occupying such little space
Isn't realistic
seeing as though nobody
will truly remember your face

So why would you choose
to NOT be who you're meant to be
And instead stand tall and set yourself free

An individual
who isn't ashamed, guilty, trapped or afraid
Can be strong and open
and have their lives so made
So by choosing to be proud
of what makes your world 'right'
YOU can express in great comfort
the dreams that take over
each night

***

There was a flow starting to present itself and I couldn't nor did I want to disturb it. There was a perfect balance I was starting to witness, with the routine that had developed and it was revolving around the Monday morning sessions with Diann and the Wednesday morning acupuncture treatment with Ralph.

Every week the acupuncture stimulated certain energies within and issues would rise to the surface. More and more I started to feel strangely calm in my discomfort and happy to simply live through everything that would come from a deeper source to flood my conscious mind during the week. By 'everything' I'm referring to: insights, clarity, suppressed feelings, past fears and future predictions. I would process through writing. But this act never proved to give me enough release. So by the weekends I'd be in desperate need of a listening ear—Diann was still the only one who was allowed to hear my spoken words. Come Monday, on the verge of eruption, I'd make my way to her place of peace with my Mam by my side and I'd unload the weight of the worries, doubts and fears. As the months slowly passed, I wasn't only unloading my despair, but I was sharing more openly the dream I wanted my life to become. After every session, I felt to have been offered a new lease of life for a day or two. Then the acupuncture treatment would again be enjoyed, resulting in a similar sequence of events as the previous week. It was an ongoing and ever-flowing routine that had evolved. And it was working! Not every week was as easy or as hard as the next. But it was going exactly as it was meant to.

The acupuncture was letting me experience more moments of peace: moments without Anna. When these moments would arise, I'd be feeling to be right in the middle of the two forces and I was balanced! I wasn't experiencing extreme torture. I was simply experiencing. I wasn't giving either force any attention. There was no analyzing, no judging, no nagging, no worrying, no doubting, not a single thing. Just simply being. These moments happened

just by giving way. They taught me that by not having any thoughts
at all, I was tapping into my heart. I was feeling balanced and
I wasn't suffering, I wasn't in pain. This, to me, was the ultimate
state of happiness! I was starting to feel how deep joy lies. By
giving way, I would sometimes be overwhelmed with sadness for
the level of self-loathe I once had owned. This sadness was just a
passing emotion. Just like every other emotion that would be rising
and falling, rising and falling, rising and falling. I didn't question
and I didn't judge. And with every rise and fall—throughout my
moments of being 'in between'—a whole new world opened itself
up to me.

I felt I was actually giving rise to my better part! What a
fantastic mathematical conclusion! The rising was at a slower
pace than the actual emotions that were revealing how little
I once loved myself. It didn't matter. I was so safe already in the
feeling that I was bringing something new to life. Something new
and improved takes precious time to become all it's meant to.
And it can only become something special when it receives the
necessary nourishment. I was practising patience. These moments
of peace literally made my soul feel full and I'd be stronger to put
the puzzle of anorexia together. I suddenly knew I couldn't fear
anything or class any revelation as being bad, because it was all
in aid of my recovery. And that simply had to be nothing less that
perfect!

I remember once saying to Diann that I felt so happy and
content in my discomfort. I wouldn't have wanted to be anywhere
else in the world other than curled up in a ball with my eyes shut,
a blanket keeping me warm and looking my inner world—in
all its former, present and future glory—straight in the eye. The
passionate traveller was suddenly travelling everywhere but not
moving an inch in space. I recall writing these exact words, when
feeling such contentment, 'The inside of me is becoming beautiful

and the expression of this beauty will come in due time.' Writing in this manner felt to initially be a sin, however I didn't care! It gave me strength and pride to have owned up to feeling beautiful, even when I despised my reflection.

This was the natural flow. Working against this flow and ignoring the 'nothingness' was something I knew would cause self-harm. After all, it wasn't 'nothingness' I was experiencing! It was sacred and needed to be valued, treasured and classed as a worthy possession. This is when it finally clicked: I wasn't invincible and I was a fragile human being (something that my indestructible false strength always had convinced me of NOT being). And if I was to forget my vulnerability I would be steered away from the freedom I was attaining within. Fay needed this freedom and was so eager to remind me as she presented such 'nothingness'! I was finally not only HEARING the wise words Diann had told me, stating, 'We aren't the emotions we feel, the thoughts we have or the behaviour we practise. Instead we are something much deeper.' Now I was FEELING it! I was slowly sensing who I essentially was.

Invisible but present

Through the thick black clouds
something becomes clear

It's the dawning of the day
or the man on the pier

Liberation is the feeling
after releasing the fear

Ego has also stepped down
and a soul can appear

An adventure into the unknown
speeding at top gear

Something more is required
a guide to help steer

Feeling happy for no reason
that's so valuable and dear

The music and the sea
are the only sounds to hear

The humming and the gushing
telling you the end is near

The peace is so powerful
it brings you one lonely but happy tear

***

By literally having gone to the bone of my existence I was now figuratively going to that exact same place. I was being stripped bare of all I once believed my self to be. No longer did I want to be looking for happiness outside of my self. I suddenly saw that I'd been trying to fill myself up with every accomplished achievement in the surrounding world, with the aim of feeling love. Yet never would my approach have led me to my heart. The place it led me to, was the truth: I felt unworthy of a space on this earth. Anorexia led me to a spot deep down that was empty of love.

Sitting in my truth, I was igniting love for life. With that, I was igniting love for myself. I was a passionate soul. I knew this, I felt this and so I used it in order to feel that same sense of devotion for what I was going through. I was going through my SELF. This meant I needed to give my SELF devotion. Devotion means love and to love is to feel worthy. I needed to start feeling worthy of my life and worthy of taking up a space on this earth. I was sitting in the perfect depth of my truth, where my sense of worthiness was starting to fill me with happiness. I knew that my passion for life was coming to the surface and the world would soon be experiencing it. My passion was no longer to be expressed in my goals, my aims or my objectives. I no longer was meant to run, to achieve, to prove nor to be everything and so much more—just to feel worthy. This was Anna's purpose. But it was no longer to be mine! I was sensing my own my soul.

I was learning that we choose to project our own self-worth to the world, through the purpose we sense. And sensing is feeling. The purpose, the intention, the heartfelt passion or the underlying desire—that's brought to the surface by being truthfully tuned in to who we are—presents a gift that's always been there. However, that gift was overshadowed by the controlling mind, society and world. We once may have given the outside world the priority in our lives, thinking we needed IT to be happy. But we learn we can only embrace the world in the desired manner, if we give our SELVES priority in our own lives, before all else. And by 'all else' I mean everything!

By being truthfully in tune, a gift is discovered and it reveals what gives us true happiness. We discover our gift for our selves first. We sense our own truth. We sense all that we are. Only then can we reveal to the world all that we are! We suddenly are living from our deepest desire and this naturally is fulfilling and satisfying. The serving of the gift and heartfelt intention is only made possible when the inside is already full. How else can we serve anything when there's nothing inside to present on a gold platter? It's not possible! And why must it be gold, when it's finally being served? A silver platter would never do the portion of oneself any kind of justice! Not if we truly love ourselves and know how valuable we are. Then, and only then, is a gold platter the way in which to dish-up as large a helping as we can muster—to the whole wide world!!!

Trapped to fly

Solitude and isolation
the ingredients for discovery

Finding the way
without motions and movement
means recovery

It's in a sense of stillness
but where adventures seem flowing
And each one contributes
to the physical and mental growing

Not going anywhere but getting everywhere, fast
The underlying experiences causing a rising blast

Locking oneself away
shows the opportunities within reach

The visions are endless
and aren't justified through speech

Seeing it and holding on so tight
as it seems pure bliss
Not letting go
is knowing that never shooting
guarantees a miss

Waiting so patiently
to express and discover every ounce
As solitude shows
that a peaceful mind encourages
that daily bounce

Bubbling and brewing
as stillness catches the world's eye

Nobody can imagine the power of letting go, in order to fly

The energy is not superficial
but of a higher form
A flutter through the core
is a sign of being reborn

Lower energy indicates a body happy to just BE
Higher energy is the source of providing natural ecstasy

Desires continue
as dreams will forever unfold
Revealing and cherishing
that existence is pure gold …

***

Needless to say, at this point on my journey, I couldn't live without writing. There wasn't a day that went by when I didn't sit tapping on the keyboard. And if I wasn't tapping, I was jotting down notes that were referring to issues I needed to address. Writing was saving me. Saying 'writing' saved me, actually means I was saving myself by wearing my heart on my sleeve and letting the world read the expression of my self. I was developing something deep as I was eating my way towards freedom. A strange concept to grasp but I found that writing was permitting me to eat! Writing was how I was dealing with the emotions that would be brought to the surface through the eating process. Suddenly I learned the basics of anorexia: I used to deal with my emotions through deprivation, restriction and ultimately starvation! And, from where I stood, I was able to see why the recovery had been so intense, when dealing with moods. Throughout the re-feeding process I felt I'd lost control. There was no more hunger. There was only food. I had nothing to cling to. So my emotional self was struck hard and my mental self wasn't unable to deal! This realization was only made after a particular incident when Anna was trying to attack. It was as if out of nowhere, I didn't want to eat! And it felt to be the strangest thing! When logic and feeling would slot together so easily, the whole illness—that once seemed too complex to ever make any sense of—instantly seemed so rational and straightforward.

By expressing myself through writing I'd taken myself on a journey that had so far already gone deep into my existence. I was no longer suppressing my emotions but I was learning to deal with them, through writing. I was figuratively feeding Fay with the words I wrote and the writing had become the way in which to deal with life. It was stopping me in my tracks, letting me regain a sense of calm control from a deeper source and I felt grounded and strong. For months it was only in my moments of writing that I'd feel worthy and I'd loose my sense of shame. Also I was gaining an inner confidence, through what I was creating. I started giving such importance to the simple flow each sentence would take and every word in the English language became so special. This passion I was discovering made me cry tears of joy. To feel such deep happiness and peace told me that this was the purpose I was serving! I suddenly knew I was recovering so I could pass on what I was gaining and help others. The words I chose to type were becoming my source and a deep passion was coming alive in the voice of wisdom I was developing—without forcing anything.

Words

A word filling each space
to build a sentence
that takes on a meaning
Each sentence contributes
to the creation of a river
that's ever streaming

It's the making of something
of an interest to maybe just one soul
It may only remain for the creator
to eventually reach that
lifetime goal

The importance can't be judged
by what the paragraphs and pages reflect
Stopping to restart the process again
in order to feel a sense of protect

Every idea that lies beneath
or every desire that is hidden or disguised
Nobody will ever know exactly the lengths
that were made for this to arise

It has a cover
just like every other
but that doesn't say it all
Claiming that's what makes it a success
is predicting a nasty fall

It's to heal a person
or to make the light shine
as brightly as it can
Pride will be already within the creator
who is also its biggest fan

A word used correctly
forming a sentence
to release and relive the event
Is never a waste of time or thought
and it's energy and devotion well-spent

The words will enrich
and the event will be embraced
to heal and discover
Which means the conclusion of the story
will be reached
one way or another

The outside says nothing
but is only an indication
as to what's behind
The soul
has been put
into a maze of different words
coming from one mind

Whatever their intentions are
or whether it be
destiny or luck
Time will reveal all
as the coincidences and twists of faith
become unstuck

The pleasure to come from something so evident
that was there all along
Shows the simplicity that feels so familiar
and words fit for a song
Being pushed to see the good and the great
by the presence
of something so bleak
Causes no shame, no guilt, no fear
and soon it's very
special and unique

***

Having the ability to face myself inside, was giving me strength to face myself outside. I'd been ignoring the mirror as much as I could. I needed to face facts, whether my lying mind would tell me I'm worthless for gaining weight, or whether my honest heart would tell me I'm safe, even whilst gaining weight. I needed to look and feel confident in my own skin, before being able to feel confident in the observing eyes of others.

I gradually urged myself to search the reflection for the love and happiness and inner confidence I'd been starting to feel. I needed to look past the skin in which I was sitting. So I consciously took to standing in front of the mirror and I'd stare into the windows of my soul. I wanted to SEE that beauty I'd been FEELING, throughout my hours of rest and writing. I wanted to SEE past the curves I was gaining, the bones that were disappearing and the cheeks I felt were way too fat. I wanted to SEE the sparks I'd been starting to FEEL. I wanted my eyes to be the witness of that energy of life!

I found that by staring into my eyes, the only thing that permitted me to FEEL the states of inner joy I'd been fleetingly experiencing, was this physical body. The body suddenly became the only thing that would give me energy and life—because without it, I'd be 'nowhere'. I'd be unable to touch, connect and express myself to others. Through the body alone, I was capable of standing tall in front of the mirror and FEELING happiness! I could only experience my soul and touch the hearts of others, if I felt comfort in nourishing the body in which I was sitting. I needed this body, this physical manifestation. And it wasn't the reflection of an illness I wanted or needed, but it was the reflection of life's energy and health! I started to experience the importance of feeling a healthy body and feeling happy whilst sitting within that healthy body. I figured if I was able to FEEL happiness so strongly—whilst standing in front of the mirror—then the only thing I would SEE staring back at me was HAPPINESS! A happy feeling providing a happy reflection! It wasn't the other way around! My reflection wasn't meant to grant me access to my happiness, but my FEELINGS were to grant me that access! I learned that I wasn't meant to rely on a happy reflection to feel happy inside! And so, if health, happiness and love for life would come from a deep level then confidence would naturally accompany my new sense of being. And with this new awareness I was gradually valuing appearance and reflection as being something deeper instead of continuing to value appearance and reflection as being something superficial.

Love the skin you're in

My body is just a parcel
it's the wrapping I've been given
Is it insignificant?
or should it have a fancy pink ribbon?
Do I love the skin I'm in
or is it hate that I wish to be disguised?
Am I being forced to see what it is
or have I just never realized?

My body is just a parcel
but it's my most important possession
It is significant
and it deserves a healthy dose of obsession
I'm the only one who can treat it right
and love it as I should
I wouldn't want anyone else to
even if they could

My body is just a parcel
however there's nothing 'just' about it
Because without it, we are nowhere
and will never be fighting fit
Through it we can show who we are
and it gets us to where we need to be
A healthy mind and soul
supports a healthy body and a healthy me

My body is just a parcel
what a silly phrase
I need to own it
and to stop seeing it as a maze

Knowing what's what and knowing what's not
That's what I have to find
in order to fill the empty spot

My body is just a parcel
a parcel I have to again learn to love
So my mind fits my body
tight and secure like a hand fits a glove

That's what I want
for them to slot together and to feel pride
for what I see and who I am
as through this life I hope to glide

***

My body was starting to tell me what I needed. I had to take this guidance and prepare the food and eat it. When there was little happening in my surroundings and I was feeling somewhat settled, I was mentally able to cope with this new sense of freedom I was reluctantly yet willingly permitting myself to take. I had to act according to my needs, whether it was making me feel good or bad.

My mind knew it was allowed to have anything it wanted and suddenly nothing was out of reach. The sky was literally the limit! All corners of the kitchen cupboards were offering me unlimited potential! The only limit was my body telling me to stop when it had been given enough food! The healthy approach towards food was finally settling. The subsiding cravings—once the barriers were down and the hunger had been cured—led me to feel less indecisive, overwhelmed and guilty!

So no longer being right in the middle of both Anna and Fay was letting me feel what's healthy and what's not. For instance, I'd feel pangs of guilt whenever I'd have brief moments of contemplation whether or not to eat according to my needs. This was a strange shift. I never used to feel guilty if I chose to sit with cravings or to not eat a feared food. But now, with the sense of gratitude growing for everything life stands for, I felt that restriction was damaging me and I was upsetting my recovery. It was all coming together with so much focus.

The barriers were down and I was eating what I needed. Along with these steps, I had to know what my reasons for saying 'no' were, whenever dealing with food. Was it because it contained too many calories or simply because I'd eaten enough? Was it because of the time of day or was it because there were people around? Was it because I was upset or because I hadn't been writing? Sometimes I wouldn't know why I'd be saying 'no', other times, I did. But I never stopped analyzing. So whenever I realized—on hindsight—that my 'no' was to support Anna then I knew for future reference I had to be stronger and act differently.

It was still difficult to see food as a pleasure. Inside I was enjoying the act of eating, but the world wasn't allowed to know! I would never speak words that would resemble pleasure in eating, since that would have been an expression of love towards my self. It was obvious to everyone that I, once upon a time, hadn't loved who I was, hence disregarding food. As it was becoming more obvious that I was growing in my own self-worth, through the act of eating, I felt this to be enough. It was too soon to actually speak words of confirmation that I was growing to love myself. Eating was—just like speech, laughter and smiles—an expression of happiness and joy in life. I still wasn't able to bring all of these factors together into one mealtime. There were no smiles to be seen on my face! It was all happening inside of me—even if it was desperate for an outlet. I called it: *BREWING OPTIMISM* that was sitting patiently … waiting to be set free!

Patience

Drifting to leave
Floating to rise
Falling so fast
Away from the prize

Soaring to reach
Gliding to rise
Flying too low
Trying to despise

Rocking to ease
Resisting to protect
Giving in to feel
Letting-go to reject

Closing to open
Shutting to protect
Curling to soothe
Trying to inspect

Sleeping to cure
Thinking to find
Releasing to resolve
Relaxing to unwind

Crying to express
Endless tears to find
Eating to clarify
And to speak my mind

Weight to gain
Patience to know
Kilos to have
A face to glow

Cheeks to fatten
Benefits to know
Waiting for the time
I can let my world grow

***

I was starting to foresee a life without Anna. And to make the increasing distance all the more real, Diann suggested I lay that part of myself to rest by writing a letter of goodbye to the presence I no longer wished to give my power to. It was one of the hardest steps throughout the journey. It was a sign that I'd once accepted her overpowering presence in order to accept her now appearing absence.

Dear Anna,

I'm trying to say goodbye. This is the hardest thing I think I've ever had to do, or maybe just as hard as admitting that you had taken over my life. I've being trying to find out why I let you in my life and take control. You were a person I would see on TV, a person I would feel sorry for and have pity on. But I welcomed you on board because I was convinced you were making me happy. You were making me the person I thought I was meant to be: skinny yet so strong and proud. But you weren't somebody to be proud of. There shouldn't be any pride in having a person like you, rule my life.

But the only person who was proud of me, was you Anna. You thought I was brilliant, you told me I could conquer anything, by having you and supporting you and letting you rule my life. You took over and I let you. But admitting this was so hard and even though I made you proud of me, I felt like a failure. You made me feel like I should be ashamed of myself. I gave you everything, but got nothing in return. I gave you my life, I gave you my strength, I gave you my power. Every minute of everyday I devoted to you. And what did you give me return? Nothing … I was willing to die for you … I would have died because of you. And you would have let me. You would have sat back and enjoyed it. You would have been so happy to see me suffer as much as possible. And I was so willing to make you so happy and proud. But it would never have reached its limits. It would never have been enough for you. When would you have told me to stop? Never ...

How dare you? Take so much away from me, without giving me anything in return ... I have never come across anybody thinking they are so worthy of just taking so much and never seeing that they have to give something in return ...

I will never forget the day I choose to get rid of you ... It was the 9th of June ... I knew you would hate it. You would hate me so much and I would pay BIG TIME for trying to get rid of you. And I did ... I was forced to give up everything, my job, my life in Holland, my sisters, my friends ... I had to leave everything behind, just to be able to fight you. It must have made you feel great, pushing me just that little bit further and making my life just a little bit harder. As if you hadn't done enough damage already, you then had to take away everything else that made me a happy person ... I hated you so much for that ...

I knew it wouldn't be easy to let you go and fight you each and every day. I could have given in, but I just didn't think you deserved it. If I wasn't allowed to be happy, then you certainly weren't. So I was ready to kick your bony little ass! I've been fighting so hard against everything you led me to believe was right. I've been fighting you to find out what really makes me happy, fighting you to see just how precious life is, fighting you to find out who I really am, fighting you to learn to love myself unconditionally, fighting you to make myself stronger. Each battle was hell, and the war isn't yet over ... But you will leave shortly ...

You did me so wrong, you led me down the wrong path, you educated me so incorrectly, you lied to me about just about everything. But for somebody who really isn't a very nice person,

I've learned from you. I know you hate me for this. I know you hate the fact that I can see a positive side to all the grief you've caused me. Sometimes I care. Other times I don't. You don't deserve for anybody to care or worry about you. The guilt that you make me feel isn't half as bad as the life you sucked out of me. So if you're trying to exercise control over me, by making me feel guilty, well it isn't going to work! Because ignoring you all those months ago when I had to start eating properly was one hundred times harder to do, than dealing with the guilt you still make me feel. You thought you were so strong, but you're not. If anything, you've only made me a better person by causing all this grief and pain. And I know that will make you angry as well … But I still don't care.

You're not a nice person, but it isn't in my nature to hate people, even though I've cursed you countless times. You did me so wrong, but I'm grateful. You made me look at my life in whole different way. You've made me appreciate things that I've always taken for granted. You've forced me to look inside and see what's really there, who I am and what I'm capable of. I don't miss the life we had together. I don't cherish the months of isolation and torture and fear. But I cherish what these months have taught me. We argued and battled and you'll be going. I was so scared to think of living a life without you, but I'm strong and am only going to get stronger by fighting you. So I thank you for making me realize just how beautiful the world is, how beautiful my family is, how beautiful my life can be and how beautiful I am. I will miss fighting you as well. You kept me on my toes, you kept me in touch with my feelings and you gave me a reason to get up each morning. But once you're gone it will just be me. Alone. I'll focus on myself and on living the life that I've been fighting for.

I'll never forget you though. Because once you're gone, I'll cherish the things you've forced me to see. You'll never control me like you used to. There's no way that I'll ever give you that power again. I'm a better person for having had you in my life and therefore you'll always be a part of me. I don't regret letting you in. And I won't regret letting you go. I don't hate you, I don't love you. I just hate what you've done but I love what I've become. So I mean it when I say, 'Thank you' ... I mean it when I say, 'I have to let you go' ... I mean it when I say, 'Goodbye' ...

6

DECEMBER 2008

The letter had been written and it ripped my breaking, healing, emptying and filling heart from within my chest. Such contradictive emotions were being experienced. After speaking the words aloud, I was no longer able to hide from the fact that death had been where I'd landed myself all those months ago. Hearing myself say the words during a session, I was clearly feeling the effects this realization had on me. There had been a time when I wasn't able to look back, because there was too much to deal with. Now I was looking and recalling the moment when I truly felt an extra power inside of me—and it wasn't Anna. On that particular afternoon in August something inside spoke these words, 'It's enough, this illness has reached its peak and it's time for you to leave.' This was a voice clearly speaking to Anna. It felt like a bolt of lightening. A single solitary moment and then it was gone. It was powerful, to such an extent, that I silently replied: 'Yes, I'll fight back.' From that point onwards, the journey started and it's where I was faced with the two doors. I chose to open the door to my soul, however dark, bleak, lost and empty it was. I had turned away from death and it was only something I was able to face, four months after the actual matter.

With the strength I'd so far gained, I was capable of reflecting. I was becoming conscious to the fact that I'd experienced something I'd only ever heard others speaking of. I'd been saved by something other than what felt to be myself. This brought many

questions of religion and faith to mind. Who was it that saved me?
Where had that extra power come from? What was happening to
me? I couldn't answer these questions at the start of the journey,
but now I was able. And my answer was plain and simple. I was
the one who had saved my self! For some, giving the credit to a
God outside of themselves (regardless of the religion), can be the
way to explain what that power is. An explanation gives a reason,
it gives something to hang on to. It's logical almost. Having said
that, I wouldn't regard this as being wrong or right—it's up to the
individual to determine from what source they gather their faith,
belief and hope in life. As for me, I'd come so far and I'd already
learned that logic wasn't the object that should be taken into
account, when dealing with a force that gives rise to something
so overpoweringly amazing. I knew that the force was ME and
nothing outside of my self. It came from somewhere without
a place or a name. It came from beyond. But it was still ME.
I didn't need an explanation—for once in my life!! Yes! So far,
I'd been analyzing every other event as it had come to pass. For
once, I trusted that I'd opened the door to my lost soul where I'd
faced my demon. It was the exact place where I found the power
I needed in order to live again. It's where I started my soul journey;
the root of the illness was simultaneously the root of recovery. The
illness had led me to death's door, which had remained closed.
I was forced to open the door to my soul, where the work needed
to start. I wouldn't have been on the road to health, without having
found the source of the illness. And that source had been found
by staying behind that door and facing the many different shades
of black I was destined to be startled by. It was a journey beyond,
commencing in a destination unknown, unseen and infrequently to
be spoken of by others. For this reason, it's a journey made through
feeling alone. Explanations and logic ceased to hold on to me with
the rising knowledge that FEELING was the only way through

which I would continue to regain full health and eventually start living a full life.

It was enlightening to feel that the one thing I wasn't urged to explain was that initial power. I was relieved when seeing the depth of this journey so clearly. Suddenly I knew why I'd get tangled, frustrated and muddled, whenever I couldn't clarify every single detail. It was due to the fact that recovery from anorexia is a SOUL journey. I was travelling somewhere that has no space and no views, but expanding space and amazing views all at once! This clarified that there would never be any absolutes! Everything is personal and it's all regarding one single soul. It's down to the individual—so it can't be explained by others. It can only be felt by the person who is journeying within. They are the only ones who can do their utmost to make sense of the depth through which they're digging. And if the individual is so desperate for explanations, then the conclusions or reflections or answers can only be based on their own better judgement and feelings. I had to trust, trust and trust some more, that my feelings were guiding me through my depths and through my soul so I could find that unique spot. My feelings would lead me home.

Home is where I was heading! Looking back, it felt like angels were guiding me. I was being taken on this soulful journey and only truly starting to witness just how amazing it was. On my great days, I was curled up, away from the world. I was engaging in things that were coming out of nowhere and I was excited in my solitude. People only became aware of my excitement through my writing; my physical body wasn't yet able to handle the energy that was inside. It was too weak to bear such an amount of life. So I happily flew in the non-physical, as I created dreams throughout those moments of bliss. They gave me more life to live for. My physical limitations never limited my imagination and belief. The ability alone to dream the unlimited life, gave me all the strength I needed. I already felt that simply breathing, simply being, with a strong throbbing heart—that was becoming the source from which I wanted to live—was the reward in itself!

Such break throughs I'd have and every single thing would fall into accord. Such perfection I saw in those moments when my mind would be resting and calm, permitting me to absorb the lessons. The WISDOM told me that if I was feeling to be rewarded for doing absolutely nothing in this life, then achievements and accomplishments would never be necessary! I wouldn't need any of these things if I was feeling happy, fulfilled and loved within myself, for just simply breathing. How free I felt when feeling these words and I never wanted this journey to end! These were the moments I felt I'd been living for and every chapter of my life felt to have been in aid of this experience. I realized that we experience pain, so we can grow through it, to eventually experience peace and joy—which is the soul and sole purpose of life! Such strange words flew from my mouth during one particular session with Diann as I literally felt I was viewing the world through the eyes of the soul.

Magic Moment

Letting the other breathe
Letting the other live
Letting the other show
what it is that you can give
Letting the other feel
Letting the other listen
Letting the other realize
that nothing was ever missing
Letting the other jump
Letting the other shout
Letting the other know
that they will always be let out

A second you or a whole you
of this you weren't aware
Some attention needed
to ease the feelings that scare
A second you or a whole you
that gives you all you need
Some attention needed
to realize your life exists of that deed
A second you or whole you
that will make you feel safe
Some attention needed
to know there's no need to escape

That extra person that's sitting and waiting
Has so much patience and hasn't been anticipating
That extra person that will always be known
Has so much joy and that will soon be shown
That extra person that stands by and observes
Has so much strength and life it deserves

A moment to see and a moment to hear
Is a moment to feel that everything is near
A moment to stop and a moment to freeze
Is a moment to sit and be at total ease
A moment to ask and a moment to answer
Is a moment to give in and become the dancer

The intention is settled and therefore will come alive
By doing what is needed which is nothing before five
The intention is settled and the rest will soon be
By letting go of everything but hanging on to me
The intention is settled and this is what one must do
By using all five senses and the intuition that is you

***

Many magic moments were so significant when giving rise to my new found energy. And they could've, would've or should've been enough to set me free from everything Anna had represented; free from judgement, criticism, fears, failing, punishment, expectations, pressure, society. And they did, in those actual moments! At the precise 'time' when Fay was rising and I was giving her life, I'd savour that freedom. But the mind still needed to be used again once I surrounded myself with commotion, chaos, society, people and, most importantly, food. Giving the mind my power after I'd been giving it to my heart, meant Anna would fire up with intensity like never before! She didn't want me to be learning or feeling anything blissful. She hated me and I would pay the price. That was fine because I was STILL learning and witnessing. It was often like clockwork; after every extreme high, I was hit with a temporary extreme low.

When engaging with food and people, thoughts of all kinds would come and hit me hard—causing me to crash and almost burn, once again. Crashing could last for a number of days. I was learning that crashing was the sign to return to my peace. I was to leave the physical surroundings so as to be presented by whatever the non-physical was willing to give me. My weapon for Anna no longer ONLY a full stomach and writing but now it was also my calm moments. Because she could do nothing other than surrender. She only surrendered after she told me lies that would force me to make myself ill again. She had to throw these statements at me, 'The ceiling that represents the pleasures in life is low, and the floor of despair is bottomless.' This of course made me envision the ceiling I was staring at, as I lay in my bed, to literally be closing in on me and the floor to be sucking me up. Fay would fight back by letting me accept that the standards Anna had set, were never to be reached. Because, if Anna had her way, the ceiling of pleasure would preferably be sitting on top of me, flattening my fat body and the floor of pain would be so far out of sight that I'd be falling forever. Fay was right: these were standards never to be reached! The ones I needed to live by were the ones I was slowly creating: standards where freedom was the fuel and where control ceased. The mind was the only thing that desired something different than freedom from that control. Without control, Anna's domineering tendencies were all in aid of nothing. Anna was fighting a loosing battle because Fay simply let it all be and was fine with exactly the way things were.

The witness of my thoughts is what I was able to become. I was teaching myself, with guidance from Diann, that our thoughts control our feelings. It's not the other way around! I learned that if the mind has been conditioned to abide by healthy and positive beliefs, based on what that individual loves and what makes them truly happy, then the feelings that person has, when living out these beliefs, are ones that generate love. Going against these beliefs, makes a person feel bad and generates everything BUT love. I suddenly saw so clearly why I'd been feeling bad for eating, for months and months! I knew that I'd be recovered—and the source of self would be embraced—if I was to feel bad when living according to Anna! Because this would show that Fay's healthy beliefs were set up in my mind and they would always stimulate me to act according to principles that would let me feel good! And so, to suddenly feel bad, would mean that Anna was in my mind! Yes! I felt to have cracked the code of my life—yet again!

At that point in time, I was desperate to control my mind. I was in the process of adopting new principles and it was like revision, repetition and recap. And I was continuously practising this healthy control, each and every day. I had to stamp those new ways into my head, let the mind be the slave and create new pathways that were based on love and love alone. I trusted that the feelings would follow suit! Fay knew that the pathways in the mind would always be there and that they frequently would appear as a temptation to Anna. But she also knew that it was actually only teasing Anna, by letting her temporarily control my days with mood swings, terror, worry and punishing behaviour. These mind games were useless. I'd come so far to never let Anna have the control she needed! Now, the logic was suddenly seeping through me! Yes! Yes! Yes! So the mind I was able to change, and I was! With this answer, I was already able to answer the question, 'Who am I?' It was dawning and becoming clear! I was no longer my thoughts, my behaviour, my Anna. I was the one thing that never changes. I was only heart, only soul, only ME.

With every logical and wholehearted insight, I was sensing the growing importance in regularly giving way to Fay, in my isolation, regardless of how extreme the lows would be. Temporarily setting myself free kept things flowing and I was expanding in all directions. My physical needs differed from day-to-day, causing different foods to pass my lips, different emotions to rise and different levels of energy to give me the ability to say either 'deal' or 'no deal' to Anna.

Eating intuitively would have often been a reason for Anna to feel extremely strong, at certain moments, because I was eating only when I was hungry and no longer according to the food plan. Therefore my calorie intake may have been less, causing my weight to drop and ultimately giving Anna some sense of pride and control. This would make it harder for me to feel at peace and to fight. Thoughts were then unstable, mind control would temporarily be out the window and the ruler of my kingdom was the dominator! Such a game I was playing, all the time—and it was all just inside the body that was now weighing… 38kgs …? I wasn't sure of the number. I hadn't been weighed for months. And the number wasn't going to make me happy anymore. Happiness was being sought in a much more gentle manner! I was changing as I was feeling more worthy of life. And food was GIVING me life, but it wouldn't always RULE my life!

I felt there was a merging starting to happen. It was as if the broken heart I'd once felt, was mending. I was healing as time was passing—be it the clock on the wall or the ticking of my heart. It, or should I say, I, was coming together. The weight was slowly gaining at an unsteady pace, my reflection was slowly losing the weight and the whale I'd once seen staring back at me was also vanishing.

However, many questions still remained. Was I able to bring into the world, all that energy, passion and love I was starting to feel? Was I physically able to deal with the world, the pressures in society and the judgement that had once been the thing to drive me into my solitude? Was I able to feel and see love in others and the world? Was I able to express myself in all that I believed I was and longed to still become? I wasn't sure. The only thing I was sure of was the fact that the flow of recovery could only head in one direction: the outside world.

Leaving Survivor-Mode

The eyes open up
and it's clear you did survive
The healing had always been the sign
you were alive

So dark were the days
and you longed for something bright
You never thought the end
could ever be within sight

But you deserve to see it
As the energy is not to grieve
Instead it's there for the process of healing
to be achieved

Not sticking to the title or idea
that surviving is all you yearned
As the knowledge is there to tell you
there's so much to be learned

Going with the flow
that the soul has secretly been taking
Not pushing against that energy inside
that's a dream in the making

The next stage is awkward, is different,
but is exciting and is new
It's the time to put into practice
all you thought would never be you

Uneasiness arises as you question your thought
but ignore your fear
Trying to listen to your intuition
as it continues to steer

To thrive once the healing is done
is definitely your destiny
So letting go of survivor-mode
will make you YOURS for eternity

To survive, to heal and to thrive
from your amazing deed
Is what is intended
and deep down it's what you need

Not to wallow in the title
but to listen to your laughter
As surviving and healing were needed
to thrive for ever after…

***

One afternoon I literally felt and saw a union between my heart and the world and everything was suddenly at my fingers tips! My heart felt to become one with the physical world, my head had given way and there were no longer any barriers between my self and the world. The emotions were enough to tell me that I was feeling nothing but amazement for this even deeper awareness I'd been given: the awareness of how significant the union between the soul and the physical world is, in order to embrace this planet in the desired manner.

Recognition came that the physical body is the bridge between the heart and the world. This reality can only truly feel to appear, when extreme opposites of restriction on a physical, mental and emotional level have been experienced. The mind had once been the cause of barriers and separation, but the heart was becoming the cause of freedom and connection.

I needed this connection with the world now that I'd connected with my self so intensely. I continued pushing myself because the energy of life inside was only able to contain itself to a certain point, before it automatically started flowing into the connection I had with my surroundings. My whole being needed to be in the world with the new sense of self that was still very much in the stages of development yet becoming more evident in the presence of others.

When I was around those who I loved, I was—without any willingness—starting to communicate, starting to open up and starting to think ahead. I was expressing more positivity in regards to the progress I was making. Complements were more welcome and I was starting to look towards my future by exploring opportunities. The tendency to jump ahead, before my body was able to sustain my excitement, was something that always threw me back. I experienced this regularly and I often took on too much too soon. By, for example, jumping on a plane to Holland for five days, or by dancing the night away (Both incidents were family celebrations I couldn't afford to miss.) My body often still felt physically sick with over-activity and sudden hunger would strike up severely making me want to collapse. But these were all lessons I needed to learn because I no longer could ignore the longing I had to place myself in the chaos of this amazing world. By ignoring that urgency, I would've been going against what I was in need of, which just so happened to be THE WHOLE WORLD! And because I was living from a deeper level, I knew the energy I had was real. It was my healthy drive and my passion for living—no matter how much pressure I was putting on myself. It was happening and it was all for the good of me.

Merging

Body and mind merging into one
The distance between is second to none
The line of division setting like the sun
It's clearly invisible or soon it will become

The thoughts are the line by which the division is made
In the light of day the merging shall fade
As the mind takes control thoughts wish they'd stayed
As the body regrets being forced to the shade

Erasing the line shows that you care
Suddenly your body is your soul and you're aware
The mind remains and your person is always there
But choosing for both is showing that you dare

The insignificance of it all should be erased
The importance should arise and then be fazed
As it's you that still remains continuously amazed
By your body that has never failed, no matter how weak or dazed

Body and mind, cherish them as your wealth
Seeing the two as one will encourage good health
Time isn't an issue but it's needed for both to melt
In a positive way for every fibre to be felt …

***

The level of my sensitivity was probably rising whilst I was growing in my strength that was proving to be invincible! I felt vulnerable but strong. The vulnerable part of my self needed protection however. So I had to learn that mental strength can be used as a guard. Healthy mental boundaries can be consciously put in place between the new found sense of self (that's extra sensitive) and the surrounding world.

Without any kind of boundaries, the stress caused by living from day-to-day, can be internalized and the method used in order to cope with the stress can be through old habits of destruction. Just one trigger from the outside world can be enough to set the old behaviour off. By learning to protect the self and to feel what the energies and the stress levels can set off within, then and only then can the individual respond healthily to the shift that's made from heart to head, especially when living life from the deeper source that places a person vulnerably in this world.

I was learning through living. Stress would instantly urge me to restrict. It would also cause confusion in regards to decision making processes that were a part of daily life. The trick was to feel what element of stress in my surroundings, had triggered the desire to restrict or the feeling of indecisive confusion regarding daily activities. Whenever the fears of food would suddenly want to control my behaviour, I'd ask myself what was going on in my surroundings that urged me to search for Anna's hand. I had to witness my thoughts as they were happening and NOT act on them—however easy and safe that would have felt. And so, relating with anything outside of myself, meant a level of protection needed to be practised.

This heightened level of sensitivity was letting me recognize if certain people in my surroundings were bearing pain and grief. If this so happened to be the case, in their presence I'd feel weak, heavy and I'd struggle to eat. Subconsciously I was inclined to absorb their energy and internalize their grief. This happened, when I wasn't strong enough or willing enough to place myself in a so-called bubble of protection that I mentally had to envision myself having (which was my boundary). Helping others in need is what I'd always wanted to do in life. That longing never left my side. But I wasn't yet capable. In those moments of being physically so affected by their pain, I couldn't heal them. Usually I would have wanted to take away their pain, release them and set them free. Usually this would have made me feel strong and happy because I'd be using the pain and grief of another soul to burden my own in an attempt to self-destruct. This of course never would've lightened their load, but it would actually have doubled the worldly misery. And I didn't want to self-destruct anymore. I didn't want to feel their pain and struggles, not if it would potentially have harmed my health. So I placed my own feelings before other's and I let go of the notion that this was a selfish act. I had to accept that my time to help others would come.

I worked on my own personal boundaries and I was finding just how vital it is to take space whenever discomfort is felt in the internal world, due to the external. My stronger sense of self was permitting me to internally control the outside world more and more. I could no longer give MORE recognition to the 'things' outside of myself than the 'things' inside. To be stable within is to be stable without. Not the other way around! We cannot control the world! We can only control our own world that sits so nicely in the amazing body that is human. There's no use in blaming society for the reactions and emotions we're faced with. Once we learn to take responsibility for those rising emotions in the presence of the world, we become the healthy controller of our own world, our own truth. And acknowledgment arises for the fact that by feeling judged, we're trying to live-up to the standards of others and not to our own and we're trying to fill in the thoughts of our surrounding world. This is impossible! Because every single person that walks the planet has a different opinion and a different interpretation of what's good and bad, what's right and wrong. And do we really give so much importance to what's going on in the heads of others, when we're happy deep down inside? No. Such importance simply vanishes once the self is healed, once the person is free from past pain and future predictions. We realize that being looked at through a million different eyes, reveals a million different sides. Isn't it then far more amazing to pour all our energies into loving those one million different sides, instead of trying to BE one million different things ALL AT ONCE? We can then nourish the soul and the unlimited potential it has as we're naturally provided with precious energy to focus only on the expression of one particular side of the self that makes life worth living. And thus, I came to realize that we need society in order to PROJECT whatever part of ourselves we wish to express and can do so, wholeheartedly, if we PROTECT ourselves from outside influences that can overshadow that sense of self.

I often tried to state in one sentence exactly what I learned during my recovery, but my excitement for EVERYTHING meant I wasn't able to settle on just one single answer. I wanted to express every aspect of my discoveries, all at once! An impossible task to fill! One word however, that had always been spoken of, with either Diann or Ralph, was the word 'balance'. I learned that life needs the healthy balance for a flow to be felt. And this flow comes from the act of GIVING to ourselves as well as to others— on every level. If we're subconsciously either giving too much or too little, some degree of suffering will be experienced. I clearly hadn't given myself enough of what I needed. I reluctantly felt to be a burden on my self and therefore on others. I'd been almost incapable of receiving graciously from those who loved me, throughout most of my life. Everything that was given, in the form of help, advice, material needs and even friendship, felt to be too much to take and I was burdening others and leaving them empty—as I had nothing to give in return. I'd never felt worthy of receiving any kind of goodness. Through self-healing I was learning to love myself and to see that I was worthy of the time, the words and the thoughts others would offer. I was learning to always give enough to myself so I was able to give wholeheartedly to others. I no longer felt insignificant. I no longer wanted to shrink to nothing. This was a thing of the past. I was recognizing what and how much I was able to give, at different times, to different people, in different situations and I used my senses to set up healthy boundaries that always placed my own needs first. And my needs had become writing and regular times to reflect in temporary solitude. This was the natural flow of life that would support me and all that I'd become through fighting the eating disorder with passion, with love and with the drive for happiness to be real and true…

Let it flow

I breathe the relief, which is only the start of what I'm feeling
As I'm blessed for having felt the power of self-healing

A strength I never knew was within me, so strong
The power came from somewhere and guided me all along

That power was me, this person as she sits right here
My own work and determination to never avoid that fear

The fear of what had passed and of what was still to come
And the grief for not being weak and not wanting to run

A word only has meaning when it's experienced to the full
And the word 'strength' now reveals its potential
and it brightens the dull

Who wants to constantly feel more grief, anger and pain?
Only those who choose to use it, whilst playing this game

It eventually makes those forgotten cells feel so alive
Always looking, searching and feeling that need to thrive

This is me: a thriver and not a survivor, at heart
It's true that those who only survive will linger from the start
The difference being that surviving is barely living
And thriving is being that potential to heal
and then start giving

I can now be so certain that living is for me
And that love has made me open my heart and feel free

A love so unconditioned and my heart beats for everyone
It also beats for me, as I've learned my life isn't done

***

I'd once posed myself with certain questions, but was unable to truthfully answer because my perception of reality had become warped and it was something I couldn't rely on. I'd once been digging for answers as to how, why and when the illness struck me but never was I certain that the answers I was filling in were accurate and real. However, I'd discovered a great deal through recovery and had already realized that everything always had been working—and would continue to do so—in perfect order, no matter how much pain had passed or was still yet to come. I'd learned to accept my pain, to accept my healing, to accept my self and to accept my life. And my life hadn't started from the point of Anna's entry. It hadn't started from the point of Diann's meeting. My life had a past and I needed to face it. My journey was no longer only in aid of putting the puzzle of anorexia together. It was now in aid of putting the puzzle of ME together, the puzzle of my whole life. Finding the pieces and slotting them into the designated gaps, was the final step in becoming truthfully at peace in my self and in life.

I was able to reflect on the fact that I had, once upon a time in my blinded oblivion, believed the illness had only been a part of my life from the moment of admittance to the family doctor. How narrow-minded of me to once have thought like this! I truly had believed the disorder was only being suffered when the world was its witness. However, the behaviour was being applied long before the point of admittance. A person may appear to be something to the world, for quite some time, but secretly they can be carrying an element of destruction within themselves and they may not even be aware. My mind had opened up and I knew what the reality of my own personal encounter with this illness had been. I was honestly seeing, speaking and processing the fact that my weight had become an issue when I was boarding the plane to Australia, two years previous. Back then, I'd left Ireland with the deepest desire of proving my abilities, through not gaining weight.

I recall to this day, the very first words Anna spoke to me. I even recall WHEN those words started possessing my thoughts. It was so clear to me—as bright as day almost. It was during one of my first days in Australia that I heard these 'truthful' words, 'You don't need food Niamh, if you're not doing anything!' And by whom had this very first statement of 'honesty' been fuelled? By the voices and judgement of what felt to be the whole world, but in actual fact was Anna. I learned that I had been carrying the potential of an eating disorder with me as I set out to travel the world!

By reliving my year in Australia, I was led to the point where I took Anna's hand as the extra guidance I needed at that stage in my life. It was on the hostel floor in Darwin. I'd hit a state of depression and was only able to get passed it by grabbing ahold of her. This gave me the ability to project happiness to the world, when really I was clinging to an illness deep down. From that point in time, everything was in aid of sustaining the power of the disorder. These revelations were starting to make so much sense. I suddenly understood why I had the black notebook. I could see clearly why I'd pushed myself to destruction in the Italian restaurant, why I'd turned off to any feelings of love I had towards a certain Italian beauty, why I'd returned to Holland, why I'd stayed in a job I hated, why I'd closed myself off in my room, why I'd still pushed to travel, why I'd set the goal of going to Mexico and why I'd decided to tour-guide for three weeks and why I'd booked that flight to Ireland… Every single decision was in aid of Anna. There was a hidden blessing in every single choice I'd made and every step I'd followed through. The tours were cancelled and I begrudgingly had returned to Ireland, faced up to my problem and started my recovery! To see the links so clearly was like I was seeing different forces at work: forces conspiring against me—so I would become ill—and forces working with me—so I would fight for my life.

I always felt, throughout my journeys, that I'd purely based my decisions on my passion to travel and to live a life of dreams. However the manner in which I travelled was for the deeper intention of sustaining Anna. I recognized that I'd been claiming to be travelling so 'full of life', when really I wasn't! When first discovering this truth, I couldn't believe it! The adventure in Australia, which I'd spoke of as being the best year of my life, suddenly appeared to be a disaster because Anna had been weighing heavy in my backpack all along! Every picture I owned projected the biggest smile! How could it be that it wasn't a true smile? How could it be that I wasn't 'full of life' or happy? This 'understanding' briefly felt to shatter the dream I'd already lived. I felt temporarily like a liar and a cheat and all my adventures stood for nothing! With this new 'understanding' I knew Anna was trying to crush the memories, just like she tried initially to ruin my dreams of travel. So this was my 'misunderstanding'! It was true that I'd been happy throughout my travels and it was untrue that I was a liar and a failure. The illness wasn't caused by the country I was travelling through or by the people I was meeting and associating with. The illness was going to strike at some stage in my life. It wouldn't have mattered how much I travelled or how many different people I'd come to meet; it was going to rise to the surface throughout my time here on earth. I'll never forget Diann's words of wisdom that sparked something off deep down inside of me, 'What better time for a force that's out to destroy, to strike when the individual is following their dream and desire to be free?' Wow! I couldn't quite believe the cheek of this illness, of this force, of this Anna!

So my memories and experiences were still my own visions of utter amazement. They started to take on a different meaning and encouraged me to always only live for the sake of feeling the freedom I naturally have access to and to use this as the fuel to fulfil my own dreams!

Mending memories

A memory, so precious
A mind, so unpredictable
A memory, so honest
A mind, so powerful

No denying, it remains
Always there, engraved
No denying, it helps
Always there, cherished

Be it good, be it bad
A memory is your possession
Be it sharp, be it distant
A memory is your creation

Their reason, they are personal
Their effect, they can motivate
Their contribution, they can teach
Their lesson, they are our reflection

Depending on the situation
A memory can help us today
Depending on our destination
A memory can lead the way
Not dwelling, not regretting
But reminiscing and reflecting
Not shouting, not crying
But wisdom and happiness

Every memory is an unforgotten lesson
Every memory gives us something
Every memory is every moment
Every memory creates a life

***

I continued to release myself from my past, by stepping further back in time. From the moment of boarding that plane to Australia in September 2006, I retraced my path and questioned my approach towards life BEFORE my adventure started. This was a time BEFORE my appearance had become so important. So I wondered: what had I valued in life, before putting any extreme focus on my health and my reflection?

When I started to travel, just after leaving college in 2004, my adventures appeared to be revolving around alcohol. To say that the alcohol was the only reason for me to have loved my travels, wouldn't be the whole truth. But it did have a big impact. I wanted to rock around the world forever. And rocking was something I believed could only be done with alcohol. The surroundings were extremely supportive of this desire (The surroundings being tourist hotspots attracting those in desperate need of a week's binge drinking—in which I was happy to partake!). The decision to opt for such environments was a result of me being made believe that I was lacking in expertise to be the professional tour-guide. College tutors and lecturers were firm believers that this person wasn't cut out for the level of professionalism required from high flying tour-guides. I was just a class clown who loved to party! Could I blame them for thinking of me like this?! No, I couldn't. Because this was the reputation I'd wished to achieve. Throughout college I'd become known for this. I was happy, vibrant, energetic, funny and I'd never decline any invitations—especially not to parties! So I'd worked hard to become known as this person and I'd succeeded in attaining the desired reputation. Why did I want to have such a reputation? It was all in a desperate subconscious attempt to be different.

Once upon a time—in the fairytale dreams I'd had as a young girl—I wanted to be unique and felt travel was the way. However in college my desire felt to be nothing of the kind! It seemed everybody had universally similar longings; every young adult wanted to travel! My longing to journey the world was so deep that the normality it suddenly appeared to represent, would never fill me with the love I'd hoped it would. So then in order to be something unique, outstanding and larger than life, I took on the task of building the reputation of a hatter gone mad. The parties and the drinking needed to fill me with that feeling of speciality, as I set out to do something 'normal': travel.

For years I tried to fill myself with something I hoped would fill me with a sense of individuality and self-worth. But I failed. Around 2005, health instead seemed to give me a better feeling. Being healthy made me feel more special. Particularly when I looked at the world around me; I saw that everyone was able to drink gallons of beer and get drunk night after night but not everyone was able to shed weight 'effortlessly'! After rocking myself unhealthily around the world for eighteen months—just after leaving college—alcohol may have been filling my stomach but not my heart. Those adventures ceased and the addictive gene that had been passed on, was trying to find the most satisfying outlet and the area where ultimate control and satisfaction could be practised. Following my Dad's footsteps—by using alcohol—wasn't the way for me. The boozing had been an experiment, but it was proving to NOT be half as satisfying as starving felt to be! So the addictive force simply released the grip it was holding on a substance that's on offer in the physical world (alcohol) and started to cling to a substance that's nowhere to be touched, but only to be felt as soon as deep willpower and determination are abused! And, voila! Like magic, the addictive gene made its shift between 2005 and 2006. From then onwards, my stomach wasn't so much filling with booze but instead was slowly being drained of food! Finally my heart felt to be filling!

Perfect! Perfect! Perfect! This was precisely how my life was meant to go! Reassessing the years gone by gave me peace and the perfection of it blew me away many times over. It showed me how prone I was to my surroundings and how impressionable I'd always been. It showed me that I'd gained confidence through the incorrect means. It also gave me acceptance of who I'd always been, or tried to be. In those moments of reviewing this movie of my life I realized that my deep desires weren't the thing I'd been following, but they'd been following me! They were with me all along—but I'd always been controlling everything through the power of my own mind. My mind had led me to experience everything, in a self-harming manner. But I still passed through every circumstance in a perfect manner so the deep passion that needed to fill my days, would be experienced! That passion was travel. It seemed to have been guiding me but really it had been lagging behind. Instead my value of being unique had taken the foreground. Now though, the value of being unique, was becoming less significant and the desire to travel, was being placed where it should have been all along: first! I'd had many times when I'd doubt if I was meant to travel (before these realizations hit home). I'd wondered if I'd ever experience the world again. But suddenly I knew that travel was most certainly my passion, I most definitely longed to do so and it was unquestionably the thing that would happen! Liberation is all I felt when I discovered that there was truth in the decisions I'd made, between the time of being a nineteen-year-old teenager and a twenty-five-year-old adult.

Hidden depths

Digging—To find a depth you never knew
Digging—To appreciate what is pure and true
Digging—To discover the person that is you
Digging—To clear the clouds covering the blue

Finding—To realize exactly what's there
Finding—To search for what you weren't aware
Finding—To answer the question or dare
Finding—To question the answer that's truly fair

Discovering—To recognize what it's like to be free
Discovering—To stay in touch with two layers of me
Discovering—To do and feel how you want to be
Discovering—To fly as high as the eye can see

***

Needless to say I continued to come up with conclusions based on past experiences, present clarity and strength, all to be interpreted through the eyes of someone who was already more free than she ever had been. I wiped myself clean of what I'd valued as a young adult. There was nothing more that could harm me and I had no shame for the way I'd lived throughout my early twenties.

I soon couldn't help but be confronted with the break-up from the two-year relationship I'd had from the age of seventeen to nineteen years. Opening up those unhealed wounds, showed me the sequence of events that were a part of the soul journey I was still undertaking. I was easily able to recall my behaviour throughout our time together and could only conclude that I never felt worthy of the love I received throughout those two years. Yet he was my all, but I was nothing. I needed him to love me, yet I couldn't accept his love, all at once! Shattered I was when he chose to split and it took me nearly two years before I could speak his name without feeling sick and five years before I could face him without reliving any of that past pain. When we split, I closed my heart off to any other person who could've potentially loved and harmed me. Back then, I swore my first love was also my last love! Serious relationships were off-limits forever. And that's exactly how the following years came to pass—I never truly opened my heart to another (even though I was prone to 'fall' so easily) for fear of pain and rejection. I was going to follow my head, so as to steer clear… forever! This, I'd been told, was the safest option and, at nineteen, I believed it wholeheartedly! Only six years later was I finally able to understand what this chapter of my life was all about.

The love I sought from my first romance—yet couldn't fully receive due to feeling worthless as a person—was a continuation of the love I sought throughout my teenage years from the potential father figure—yet didn't feel to have received due to feeling unaccomplished. I needed to feel love so as to make myself complete. When I say 'complete', I'm referring to the masculine and feminine energies within the psyche that need stimulation from the outside world, through parenting. During childhood years there wasn't a vital amount of masculine energy in my surroundings to positively develop my own male energies within. As a teenager my step-dad became the one who I wanted to feel love from so as to become complete. I believed that by trying to live up to his standards, I'd receive that love. So I applied his principles as much as I could. This meant I was to have a focused, decisive, strong and powerful approach towards life. I needed to rise to the level of his living, in order to reach his love. I never did. I never succeeded and I felt that I had failed. The conclusion I found was that I was undeserving of love. By having set such a pace for myself, the course of my life had also been set. And I would go through life always aiming to achieve and prove myself worthy of that love. His presence encouraged me to be accomplished and perfect, all in the name of love. I was giving evermore power to the masculine principles. I was experiencing an imbalance and burying the natural feminine energies within and suppressing that side of myself, more and more.

Even before my step-dad arrived on the scene, I'd already believed that my purpose in life was to search for approval. Without approval I felt I had no purpose and no love. There was nothing real to live for without aiming to achieve something. Why would a person live without seeking and feeling accomplishment? If that's all there is in life then that HAS to be the only source of EVERYTHING!

Where did this need come from? I stepped back even further in time to when I was a child. I saw how strong an urgency I had to heal and take away the pain of others. I once believed I could achieve that by putting a smile on the faces of loved ones around me, especially my Mam. How did I try to make her happy? How did I attempt to heal her soul? I did so, by aiming to be accomplished and perfect. This is how I tried to take away her pain and I strived to make myself feel good. Simultaneously. Like magic! But really I was taking on the responsibilities of the world.

To let go of the desire to heal others was to also let go of the desire to achieve perfection and to accomplish goals. And by releasing these issues, I was in actual fact releasing Anna!

When coming up with this mathematical conclusion, both logic and feeling were of the essence. I was blown away by the susceptibility of each person and the way in which we can internalize the surroundings, from such a young age. I was also amazed for this internalization to be the pace a child sets for themselves and for that set-pace to then be their drive and guide throughout their time here on earth. Although the set-pace may not be the guide forever—not if the individual is driven to encounter an experience that forces them to heal childhood wounds and to change their pace. I was one of the 'lucky' individuals who had been guided to a place and an experience where I was forced to heal my wounds and to change my pace. Because approval and achievement had always been my way and it was an energy that would ultimately lead me to the illness, all with the purpose of setting me free!

Layers and layers

Underneath it all a person emerges
Who had remained unseen
You are the one that knows the importance
And what it will eventually mean
Who does what with this or that
Is a choice that only one person can make
The person this regards
Knows that deep down everything is real
and nothing is fake

Trying and trying, searching and searching,
As each day turns into another
Nothing to loose and everything to gain
As the journey is to reveal and recover
It's all in there but who chooses to see it
And when it's seen to where it should lead
You'll know the answers
If you nourish the growth
of what once started as a seed

What a person wants
Doesn't determine what's right, wrong, good or bad
It's only the essence of the truth
That will make you feel everything but sad

The real thing is within sight and reach
As it's right there for the taking
It turns out to be an adventure to grasp
And therefore a miracle in the making …

***

I felt like the innocent child again, who had been stripped bare of the beliefs stating that achievement was the necessity of life. So, without wanting or needing achievement and approval, what was in my heart?

I recalled the memory from when I was seven years old and this was my vision: I stand in front of my Dad who has just returned from travels. A dream life is what I see. He travels the open road. He's as free as a bird. His life revolves around excitement. I gaze up at him and I too want that life so much. I feel proud that he's my Dad because of his courage and strength and sense of adventure. His approach fills me with admiration and he can never do wrong in my eyes, just for the fact that he is experiencing the real life by travelling and doing something different than those around me.

As I perceived my past through the eyes of a twenty-five-year-old 'child' I acknowledged that, back then, I was unconditioned yet impressionable. I wasn't dreaming of travel in order to feel accomplished or to be approved of by life and society! I simply wanted my life to be a magical dream—and that dream lay only beyond! It didn't lie within the walls of our homely environment. So it was almost unreachable, untouchable—yet I knew it was out there. I needed for travel to give me that freedom so I could move beyond. With the influences from my Dad as well as the literal move from Ireland to Holland, at the age of nine, I'd received all the confirmation I needed: freedom lies within travel alone! The society in which I was inevitably placed, as well as the beliefs and the conditioning I was experiencing, buried that person who was sitting deep within, waiting to be brought to life, by some force or another. Meaning, there was an unrecognized and unavoidable suppression of the need to express my self without proving, achieving, shaming, failing or fearing. Suddenly I knew there was only one force that held the power to strip me bare of everything

I believed I was, in order for me to give life to who I truly felt to be. It was the force of anorexia.

With the puzzle of my life feeling to fit so perfectly, issues resolved themselves and the fire that was burning inside was ready to be set alight within the world. The self was finally being found! The suppression had been taken away and my soul was now free to express. I was suddenly right back to basics, at my core, my roots, my all. I was the innocent child again. I knew exactly who I was and what I needed to do in this life. I had reversed the cycle back to where it had all started and I was suddenly feeling complete!

Every single thing I'd come to learn through recovery was in aid of becoming complete as a person, and the love I'd once been searching for had been found within my self. I knew I'd never search for love outside of my self. I'd never fear rejection because it wouldn't lessen me as a person. I'd go through life expressing acceptance and I'd be honest and open in the love I'd feel for myself as well as for others. I wouldn't project behaviour that would be an indication of self-destruction. I'd healed my past. I'd relived and released the pains and I'd seen why I'd become so ill and I'd also seen how I'd rebuilt myself, through the power of ME.

With these insights, I gained a sense of freedom I never before felt so intensely. I needed to travel and I was the expressive writer! There was no more suppression of the dreams I was longing to live because I was flying high in the certainty of the unknown journey ahead. I'd discovered the deep passionate writer and it was all through the physical road I'd first travelled upon followed by the non-physical road. It was all in aid of showing the depth, the purpose, the self-worth, the love, the soul and the life—all so I could reach this very moment! Through writing and travel alone, I knew that my physical world—as well as my non-physical world—would continue to expand. Because from the age of twenty-five I could safely say, 'I'd be forever FEEDING, I'd be forever FAY, I'd be forever FREE!!!!!!!!!!'

Seasons after seasons

As the strong gusts of wind
once blew a cold and forceful gale
And the pain on my cheeks
was caused by each individual falling hail

With the sleet creating a blizzard
to instantly frighten
And the vision so blurred
that nothing would seem to brighten

The clouds were once so dense
that nothing was as it seemed
And the haziness I thought was my life
had to be redeemed

Every gust was my emotion
Every hailstone was my fault
Every blizzard was my fear
Every cloud was my own personal assault

Combine these conditions
to create an unforeseen weather forecast
To predict the life that could have been my future
but is now my past

No longer can the prediction be relied upon
so I give up my trust
And I'll let each pressure front take its course
as it's simply a must

As the faint light and distant breeze
have now become my surroundings
And the warmth can be felt
with the spring in every heartbeat that's pounding

With the blue skies above
giving brightness to my days
And the vision is now clear
for as far as my mind will let me fill my gaze

The clouds are now a sign of more light and clarity to come
And the haziness is not consuming my world
as it is now filled with fun

Every breeze is now my wisdom
Every heartbeat is now my strength
Every blue sky is now my love
Every light shows never-ending length

Combine these conditions
to create an unforeseen weather forecast
To come up with the sum of my present bliss
that will continue to last
And no longer to predict the future
by grasping on to seasons gone by
But by embracing the new
and trusting this feeling that I'm now able to fly

***

Epilogue

Standing in front of the mirror, sixteen days into the new year of 2009, I stared at my reflection with tears streaming down my face and the weight of the world was, once again, sitting on my shoulders. Depressed is what I felt. I felt I couldn't keep the process of recovery going in the same way anymore. I was getting stronger, weaker, stronger, weaker. I needed something more.

I stood and I looked at my reflection. I looked deep into my eyes and asked the question, 'What is it I truly need right now?' I asked for the answer to come to me. I wanted honesty in terms of my current needs. The answer was to be for the self that was only newly facing the world. I gazed past my puffy red eyes and the expression of sorrow and felt the inner love that needed to be set free and the happiness that was now my state of being. Then, out of nowhere, I said out loud, 'I have to go to Australia.' And that was that! The words had been spoken and, even though no one was there to hear me or to witness this revelation, it was enough for ME to have been the witness of my own truth, of my own promise, of my own needs. It was a confirmation FROM my heart, TO my heart. The depression fell away, a sense of calm spread through me and I was light in the certainty that I had made this decision, independently.

From that day onwards recovery was taken to a different level—a higher one. Anna was no longer being called Anna. Fay was no longer being called Fay. Anna was simply called a force of control and Fay, was... I.

The date was already set in my mind. By the end of April I would board a plane to Australia. This gave me three months in total to get myself physically strong enough and to settle into my new ways as I was putting Anna slowly to rest. The approach I took towards making the dream a reality was in a most present and mindful manner: without fear, stress, worries or attachment when trying to predict how the future was going to unfold. I was living in the moment so the experience towards making the dream come true, was being embraced. This was my reassurance that the last leg of my journey towards full health and towards Australia was also a 'leg' I'd learn and grow through, in leaps and bounds, just like every other. With every single solitary act I took, I was putting my new values and beliefs into practice and life was flowing through me. Because all that needed to happen, happened!

Stepping towards Australia, started with the first steps I took in January (seven months after being diagnosed). I literally opened the front door and walked fifteen minutes around the block— longer or further wasn't yet possible. I had to rebuild my physical body and push the boundaries eagerly yet ever so gently. I took yoga lessons, practised daily meditation and made a few weekend trips to visit some travel friends so as to get the feel for physical movement again, before setting off. I was stable around food and it often excited me! However, I knew that life would challenge me and that the destructive pathways would always be there. But I wasn't scared anymore because I had my tools, my foundations and my strength. I knew what the food issues had been in relation to, I knew the signs I had to look out for and I knew how to act if and when they'd appear. I couldn't let a potential relapse hold me back. My so-called fat days were a thing of the past. My weight could have still been gaining but I didn't know, because I didn't use the scales and it wasn't an issue! The only thing that was an issue was my life! And I was living! I was eating for life, no matter what challenges would arise or what emotions would try to unbalance me inside! I had my pen in my pocket, my notebook on hand. Nothing was going to hold me back! Not even the door to my life in Holland—that was still on a latch. I had to close this door during this period. So I resigned from my old job at the travel agency and I gave up my bedsit. They both had been waiting for me throughout my recovery in Ireland. I was closing those doors. I was unburdening my soul by distancing myself from a place that felt to have suppressed me throughout various stages of my life. I was no longer comparing myself to my friends, who lived in security. I was secure within myself and that was all I needed. I accepted a life of uncertainty, a life of freedom. It's all I ever longed for, ever since staring admiringly at my Dad for the life he lived. So I thanked Holland for all the lessons, experiences and people it brought me. I carried those people safely in my heart and I stepped away.

Those who had supported me may have felt this step to have been too much, too soon: hopping on a plane to the other side of the world only ten months after knocking on death's door. This was due to them suddenly witnessing the actions I was taking in the physical world, as I was starting to embrace life again. Throughout other stages of recovery nobody was an eye-witness to anything; I was working within. This stage of recovery was without. In reflection, all stages were going at a speed that often blew me away, so this one wasn't any different. Either way, I didn't need anybody's approval. The voices of the world had once subconsciously controlled me, but this would no longer be the case. All I needed was to follow my heart. Mam believed in me so strongly and supported my every step. Although she needed to come to terms with the speed of my recovery, in her own way. Still her backing and Diann's vote of confidence were enough for me to realize that I could make anything happen. Why had Diann's voice come to hold so much importance for me? At this stage of my recovery, I was able to witness the profound effect she, as a person, had on me. Her belief in me felt to be my truth. As clarity was dawning, my own intuition was strengthening and my voice was getting louder. However, for so long, she had been my voice. Whenever questions would arise in my mind as to what the deeper meaning behind my thoughts and actions could have been, I literally would hear her words. I would hear her pose me with the exact same question, but in a manner that could only lead to the answer being good and positive and always for the benefit of my truth and my health. It dawned that, due to her guidance, I'd developed the ability of speaking to myself as the outsider who had life experience and wisdom without end. She had represented my truth from the word 'go'. What a gift to have her voice with me at all times, whenever it needed to be called upon.

Diann supported me and I didn't need to explain to her why Australia was where I needed to go. But to others, I automatically did. People wondered why I was going back to the country where anorexia had taken ahold on me. This was something I couldn't answer. Maybe it was to lay the past to rest. Maybe it was to look at the country through different eyes. Maybe it was a point from where I needed to start travelling the world again. I couldn't give the exact reason. All I knew was that I had to go. I trusted myself more than ever before. With this trust, I knew I wasn't racing around the world. I didn't long to be different or to be approved of and I didn't need to run from any fears or unresolved past issues. I didn't need to achieve and I wasn't being driven by judges in society or by a judge inside my own mind. I'd discovered my true desire, and yes, it was travel. In my heart, travel and life held the same meaning. My home I'd already found. It was within. I'd once searched the world to find the happiness that can only be found inside. My travels did eventually bring me both—happiness and home—but it was through a far different route than I ever imagined!

When it came to bidding my support system farewell, I realized how much closer a connection I'd formed with every single person in my life. 'Endless gratitude' and 'forever in debt' were the terms that would come to mind when realizing the concern they'd expressed. These words weren't for a sense of feeling non-deserving of what they had been giving me. These words of appreciation were instead fuelled by the love I felt towards myself for all that I'd become. I knew that without their support, my journey would never have been the same. And I wondered if I'd ever be able to repay them. All I had given them were half a million words. I'd given them the words that were stored away on my lifesaving blog, all representing a particular level of my self. That's where my love for life, for my family, for my friends lay. They saw my repayment for what they'd given me, as my life in itself. Regardless of the fact that it would temporarily be on the other side of the globe. The connection that had been strengthened I knew would benefit us always, especially as I was travelling once again. I'll never be able to give thanks for the understanding, acceptance and love they showered me with, throughout. Professionals that were called upon, being Ralph and the family doctors Siobhan and Nick, were compassionate and supportive without bounds. They unknowingly held an essence of my healing in their approach. As for Diann: the lessons she taught me, the guidance she gave me and the freedom she offered was, and still is, too much to ever put into writing within the pages of this book. I'll never be able to show her the level of gratitude and love she deserves for giving me the life I now live. And this exact same expression I use in relation to my Mam. In addition I say—from the depth of my being—that she is the one who opened Diann's doors. My Mam brought me towards her light and by doing so, she ultimately gave me my second chance to live and to be free.

My two angels, who are always safe with me, wherever I may go, wherever I may flow...

The main thing I learned throughout the recovery is that dreams can become a reality by tapping into the inner potential and holding on to the bigger visions. This was a most important element that kept my recovery ongoing. I'd been trapped for months but I was dreaming of beyond all the time. And finally I was starting to make that dream a reality, throughout the three months of preparing for Australia. That special date of April 23rd 2009 came and I boarded that plane. This is when I realized that all we must do in life is believe in the dream that may feel to lie far beyond, but is way closer than we can ever imagine—because it sits within our heart. We have that power to unleash the beast and to go for gold. Because we already are gold! Every single person— that even goes for me.

Anorexia brought me to my depths where I found what I truly, madly, deeply desired to do! I made it to Australia by the date I'd set, with my pen in my hand and with love in my heart. I managed to beat all the odds, when people were thinking I was taking on too much. I put myself into the world and I placed love first, Niamh second and life followed! The magic unfolded and adventures were all I had. I put into practice the lessons I learned and I followed the universe with every intuitive nudge that came from within and I grew even more. I used the world as a place in which to express my self and it became my playground. And guess what? It still is and therefore forever will remain that place of playful expression!

Travel brought me home and, as my repayment, I shall always bring travel home to me.

One last verse

Look up at the sky
and see that star
Jump up and be it
is an achievement by far

Reach out and touch them all
as it is your right
Open your arms and hug them
it's the end of the fight

So spread your wings now
and join those skies
See there are no more limits
as beyond is where it lies

Where it will lead
only the universe can know
But one certainty remains
that this star is ready to go …

One more tear that is shed here today
Just one more
for the joy of forever being Fay